teach® yourself

**quick fix
excel 2002**

teach®
yourself

quick fix
excel 2002
stephen morris

For over sixty years, more than 40 million people have learnt over 750 subjects the **teach yourself** way, with impressive results.

be where you want to be
with **teach yourself**

For UK orders: please contact Bookpoint Ltd, 130 Milton Park, Abingdon, Oxon OX14 4SB. Telephone: +44 (0) 1235 827720. Fax: +44 (0) 1235 400454. Lines are open 09.00–18.00, Monday to Saturday, with a 24-hour message answering service. You can also order through our website www.madaboutbooks.co.uk

For USA order enquiries: please contact McGraw-Hill Customer Services, PO Box 545, Blacklick, OH 43004-0545, USA. Telephone: 1-800-722-4726. Fax: 1-614-755-5645.

For Canada order enquiries: please contact McGraw-Hill Ryerson Ltd, 300 Water St, Whitby, Ontario L1N 9B6, Canada. Telephone: 905 430 5000. Fax: 905 430 5020.

Long renowned as the authoritative source for self-guided learning – with more than 40 million copies sold worldwide – the *Teach Yourself* series includes over 300 titles in the fields of languages, crafts, hobbies, business, computing and education.

British Library Cataloguing in Publication Data A catalogue record for this title is available from The British Library.

Library of Congress Catalog Card Number: On file.

This edition, first published in UK 2003 by Hodder Headline Plc, 338 Euston Road, London NW1 3BH

First published in USA by Contemporary Books, A Division of the McGraw Hill Companies, 1 Prudential Plaza, 130 East Randolph Street, Chicago, Illinois 60601 USA

The 'Teach Yourself' name is a registered trade mark of Hodder & Stoughton Ltd. Computer hardware and software brand names mentioned in this book are protected by their respective trademarks and are acknowledged.

Typeset by Butford Technical Publishing, Pershore, England.
Printed in Great Britain for Hodder & Stoughton Educational, a Division of Hodder Headline Plc, 338 Euston Road, London NW1 3BH by Cox & Wyman Ltd, Reading, Berkshire.

Impression number   10 9 8 7 6 5 4 3 2 1
Year   2007 2006 2005 2004 2003

contents

01

using excel worksheets

Load Excel

You can run Excel in a similar way to any other Windows application:

1 Click on **start**.

2 Move the pointer to the **All Programs** option.

3 Move the pointer across to **Microsoft Excel** and click.

Excel is loaded and the main Excel window is displayed.

You can also run Excel by double-clicking on the Excel icon on your Windows desktop (if one was installed).

Use the Excel display

The Excel display contains all the usual Windows components.
These surround the grid, where you enter and edit data.

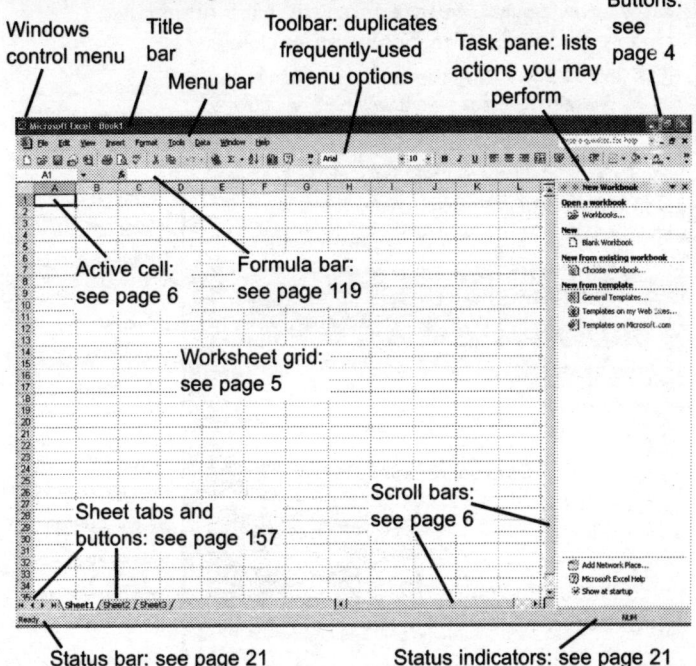

Windows control menu

Title bar

Menu bar

Toolbar: duplicates frequently-used menu options

Task pane: lists actions you may perform

Buttons: see page 4

Active cell: see page 6

Formula bar: see page 119

Worksheet grid: see page 5

Sheet tabs and buttons: see page 157

Scroll bars: see page 6

Status bar: see page 21

Status indicators: see page 21

Use the window controls

The Excel window can be maximized, minimized or closed. Data is
displayed on a worksheet window, inside the main Excel window;
this window can also be maximized (so that it fills the Excel
window), reduced in size, minimized or closed.

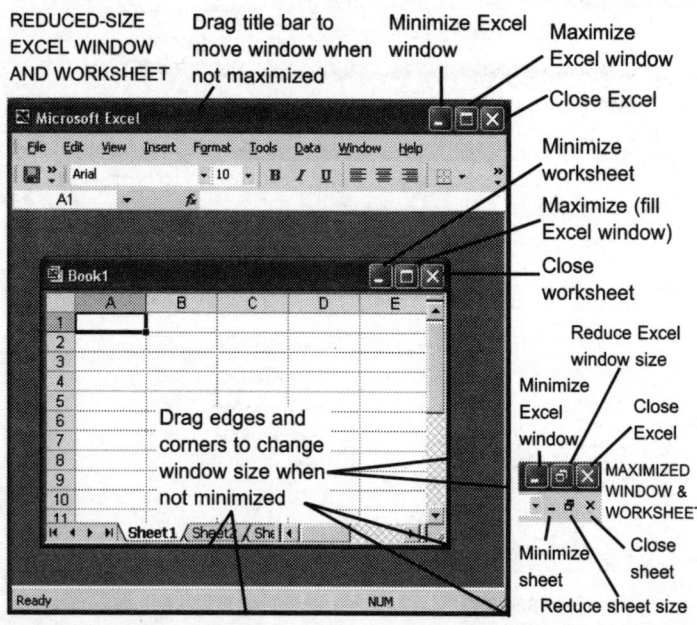

REDUCED-SIZE
EXCEL WINDOW
AND WORKSHEET

Drag title bar to
move window when
not maximized

Minimize Excel
window

Maximize
Excel window

Close Excel

Minimize
worksheet

Maximize (fill
Excel window)

Close
worksheet

Reduce Excel
window size

Minimize
Excel
window

Close
Excel

MAXIMIZED
WINDOW &
WORKSHEET

Minimize
sheet

Close
sheet

Reduce sheet size

Drag edges and
corners to change
window size when
not minimized

Identify worksheet cells

The worksheet consists of labelled rows and columns, forming a grid of cells. Each cell can contain one item of data (a number or a piece of text).

- Columns are labelled A to Z, then AA to AZ, BA to BZ, etc. There may be up to 256 columns (the last being IV).

- Rows are numbered from 1 at the top down to a maximum of 65536.

- Each cell is uniquely identified by a reference consisting of the column label and row number (e.g. A1 for the top left corner cell).

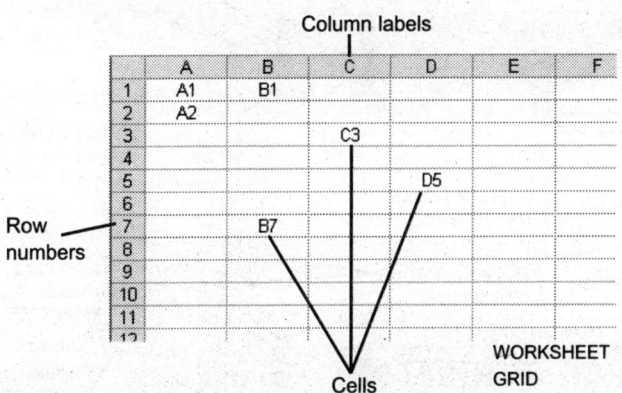

Column labels

Row numbers

Cells

WORKSHEET GRID

Change the active cell

One cell on the worksheet is identified by a thicker border. This is the *active* cell, where you can enter and edit data. Only one cell is active at any one time.

You can make any cell the active cell as follows:

- Click on another cell.
- Use the arrow keys to move to another cell.
- Press **[F5]**, enter a cell reference and press **[Enter]**.

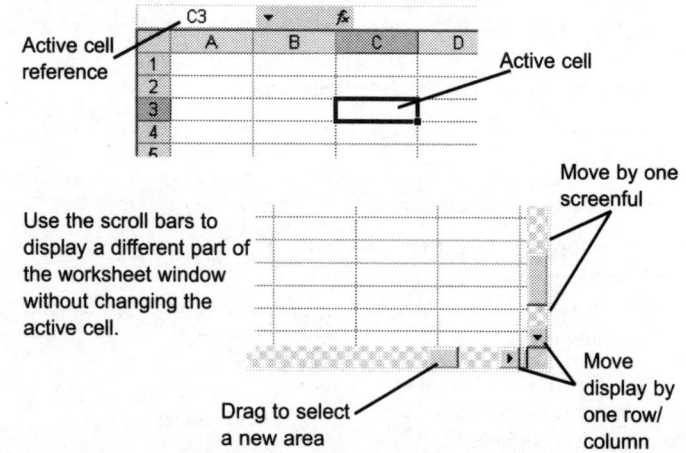

Active cell reference

Active cell

Use the scroll bars to display a different part of the worksheet window without changing the active cell.

Move by one screenful

Drag to select a new area

Move display by one row/ column

Mark ranges

A *range* consists of a rectangular block of cells, identified by the cells at the top left and bottom right corners, separated by a colon.

Ranges

	A	B	C	D	E	F	G	H
1								
2		B2:B2			D2:F2			
3								
4								
5				B4:F6				
6								
7								

To mark a range do one of the following:

- Drag the pointer from one corner to the opposite corner to mark a block.

- Click on a cell to mark it.

- Click on a column letter to mark the whole column or a row number to mark the whole row.

- Click on the square in the top left of the worksheet to mark the whole sheet.

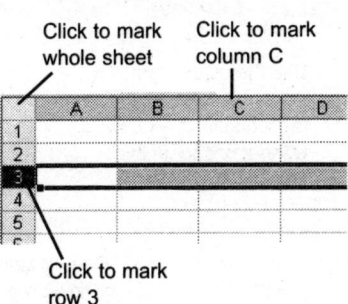

Click to mark whole sheet   Click to mark column C

Click to mark row 3

Close Excel

Close Excel in any of the following ways:

- Click on the ☒ button in the main window.

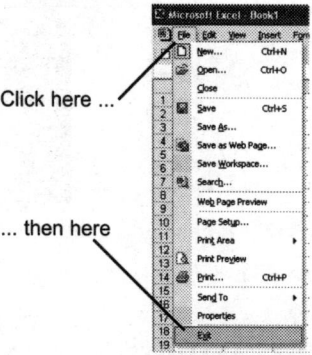

Click here

Click here ...

... then here

- From the **File** menu, select **Exit** (or press [**Alt**] [**F**] [**X**]).

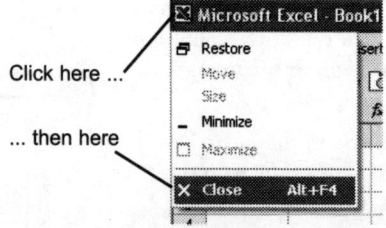

Click here ...

... then here

- Select **Close** from the control menu (or press [**Alt**] + [**F4**]).

02

on-line help

Use the Office Assistant

The Office Assistant is an interactive help tool, which appears on your screen when you ask for help using the **Microsoft Excel help** option from the **Help** menu.
(You may have to turn this feature on – see page 12.)

You can use the Assistant to answer a particular query.

1 Click anywhere on the Assistant. You are asked what you want to do.

2 Type a query into the box.

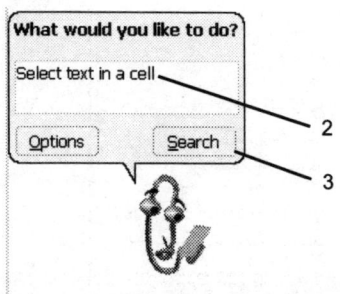

3 Click on **Search**. A list
   of possible matching
   topics is shown. If
   necessary, click on **See
   more** to list further
   topics.

4 Click on one of the
   topics. The Help window
   is displayed. Increase the
   window size if necessary.

5 Click on the ☒ button
   to close the Help window.

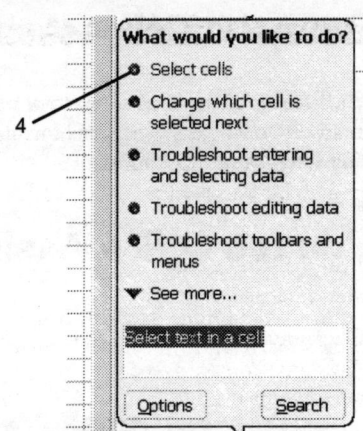

What would you like to do?

- Select cells
- Change which cell is selected next
- Troubleshoot entering and selecting data
- Troubleshoot editing data
- Troubleshoot toolbars and menus
▼ See more...

Select text in a cell

Options   Search

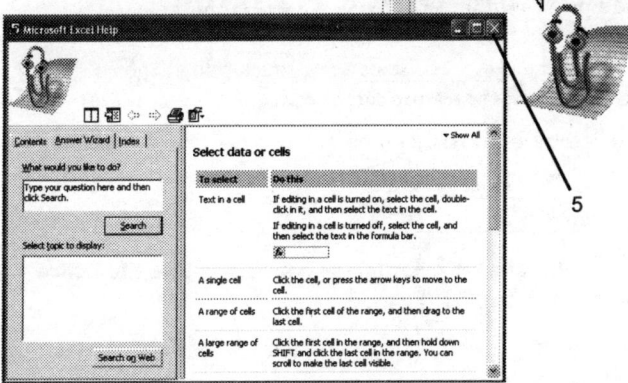

Microsoft Excel Help

Contents | Answer Wizard | Index

What would you like to do?

Type your question here and then click Search.

Search

Select topic to display:

Search on Web

Select data or cells   ▼ Show All

To select	Do this
Text in a cell	If editing in a cell is turned on, select the cell, double-click in it, and then select the text in the cell.
	If editing in a cell is turned off, select the cell, and then select the text in the formula bar.
A single cell	Click the cell, or press the arrow keys to move to the cell.
A range of cells	Click the first cell of the range, and then drag to the last cell.
A large range of cells	Click the first cell in the range, and then hold down SHIFT and click the last cell in the range. You can scroll to make the last cell visible.

Show the Office Assistant

If the Office Assistant does not appear on your screen, or has been turned off completely, display it by selecting **Show the Office Assistant** from the **Help** menu.

Hide the Office Assistant

To remove the Office Assistant from your screen, select **Hide the Office Assistant** from the **Help** menu.

Turn off the Office Assistant

After hiding the Office Assistant a few times, you are given the option to turn off the feature completely.

You can also turn the Assistant off at any other time.

1 Click on the Office Assistant.

2 Click on **Options**.

3 On the **Options** tab, click on the box next to **Use the Office Assistant** (to remove the tick).

4 Click on **OK**.

Change the way the Office Assistant works

You can change various options that affect the operation of the Assistant or the type of information it provides.

1 Click on the Office Assistant.

2 Click on the **Options** button.

3 On the **Options** tab, click on the check boxes to turn features on or off.

4 Use the **Gallery** tab to select a different animation.

5 Click on **OK**.

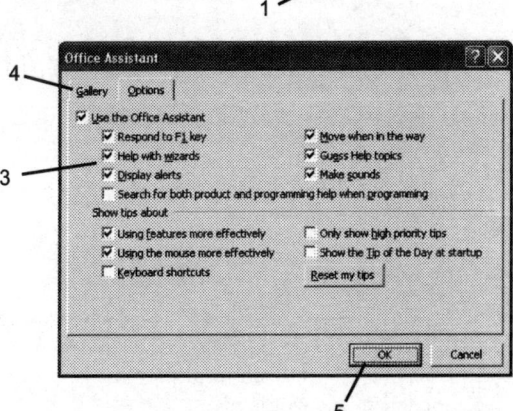

Office Assistant

Gallery Options

☑ Use the Office Assistant
  ☑ Respond to F1 key   ☑ Move when in the way
  ☑ Help with wizards   ☑ Guess Help topics
  ☑ Display alerts   ☑ Make sounds
  ☐ Search for both product and programming help when programming

Show tips about
  ☑ Using features more effectively   ☐ Only show high priority tips
  ☑ Using the mouse more effectively ☐ Show the Tip of the Day at startup
  ☐ Keyboard shortcuts   Reset my tips

OK   Cancel

Display the Help window

You can get on-line help directly from the Excel Help program.

1 Turn off the Office Assistant completely (see page 12).

2 From the **Help** menu, select **Microsoft Excel Help**.

   Or

   Press function key **[F1]** or click on 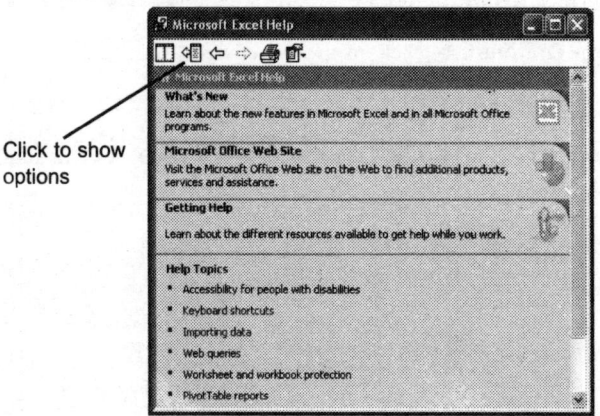 on the toolbar.

Click to show options

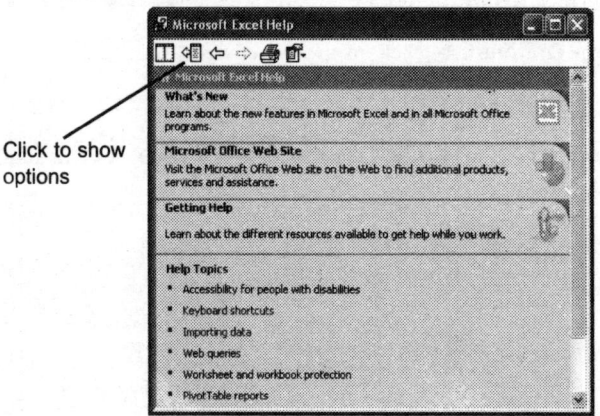

3 Click on the button to display the help options in a pane on the left of the window.

Select a help topic

The Excel help topics can be displayed by clicking on the
Contents tab. The topics are arranged as a series of books, some of
which contain other books.

- Click on the ⊞ symbol to open a book.

- Click on the ⊟ symbol to close a book.

- Click on a topic to display the corresponding help text.

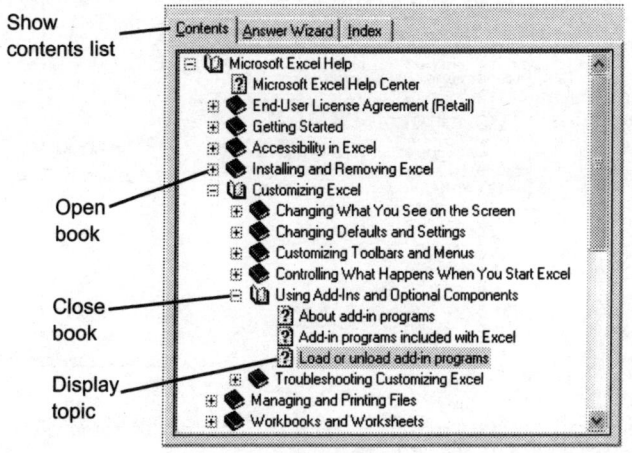

Show contents list

Open book

Close book

Display topic

Jump to a related topic

From within the help text, you can jump to related help topics.

- Click on underlined text to jump to help relating to that phrase.

- Click on coloured (but not underlined) text to see a description of that phrase – a *glossary* entry.

- Click on an item with a right-pointing arrow at the side to show more detail.

- Click on an item with a down-pointing arrow to hide the extra detail.

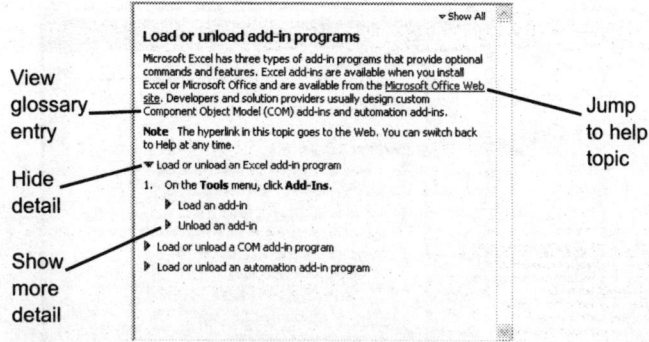

When you have viewed a topic once, the links to that topic are shown as purple rather than blue text.

Search for help with the Answer Wizard

You can search for help on a particular subject in two ways. The first method is similar to the Office Assistant approach:

1 Click on the **Answer Wizard** tab on the Help window.

2 Type a query in the upper box.

3 Click on the **Search** button.

4 Click on one of the topics in the lower box.

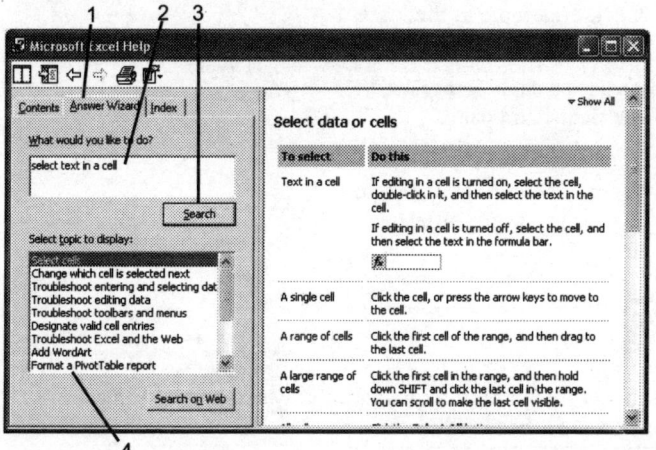

Search for help using the index

The help index lists key words and phrases in the help text.

1 Click on the **Index** tab in the Help window.

2 Type a word in the top box.

Or

Start typing a word and then click on the required keyword in the middle box.

3 Click on the **Search** button.

4 Click on a topic in the bottom box.

The selected topic is displayed in the right-hand pane.

Sometimes the word you want does not appear in the index, so try equivalent words or related topics.

To see where the selected topic is in the help hierarchy, click on the Contents tab.

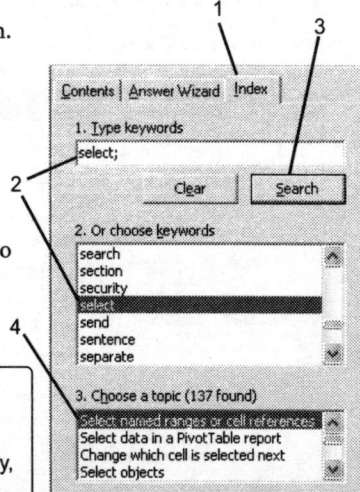

Contents | Answer Wizard | Index

1. Type keywords

select;

Clear | Search

2. Or choose keywords

search
section
security
select
send
sentence
separate

3. Choose a topic (137 found)

Select named ranges or cell references
Select data in a PivotTable report
Change which cell is selected next
Select objects

Use the Help window options

The buttons at the top of the Help window allow you to move around the help topics and perform other operations. You can:

- Resize (tile) the help and Excel windows to fit the whole screen.
- Hide (or redisplay) the left-hand pane, containing the tabs.
- Go back to the previous help topic you selected.
- Go forward again to the next help topic.
- Print the current help topic.
- List other help options.

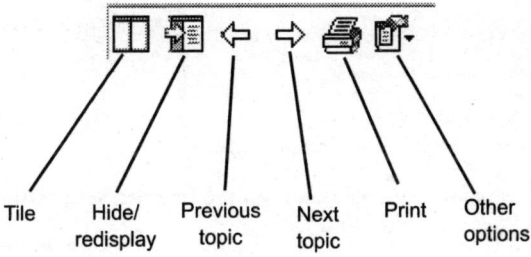

Tile   Hide/   Previous   Next   Print   Other
        redisplay   topic   topic   options

Use other help facilities

Excel provides some other useful facilities that help you use the program:

- If you place the pointer over a toolbar button, after a short pause a label pops up to tell you what the button is.

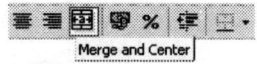

- For more information about any object on the Excel display, select **What's This** from the **Help** menu and then click on the object.

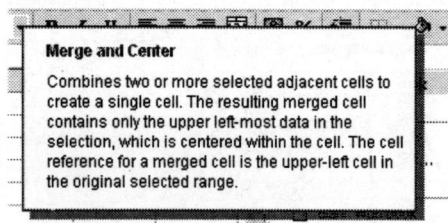

- For information from Microsoft on the Internet, select **Office on the Web** from the **Help** menu.

- For version number and product ID information, select **About Microsoft Excel** from the **Help** menu.

Use the status bar

The status bar at the bottom of the worksheet window displays messages as you are working with Excel.

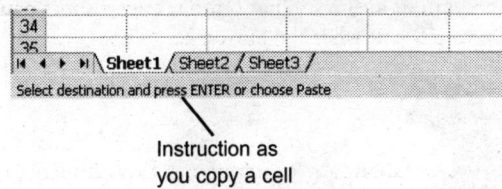

Instruction as
you copy a cell

The right-hand side of the bar has a number of indicators that give you information about the worksheet and your computer.

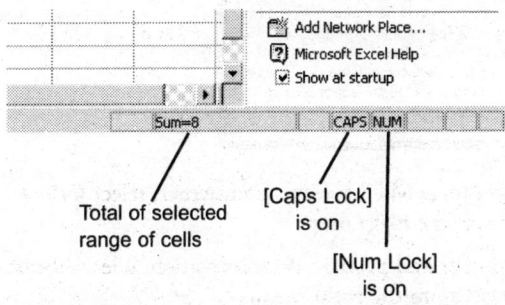

Total of selected
range of cells

[Caps Lock]
is on

[Num Lock]
is on

03

entering data

Enter a value in a cell

Each cell on the worksheet can hold a single value.

1 Click on a cell.

2 Type a value (a number, a date or a piece of text). The value is displayed in both the cell and the formula bar.

	C2		▾ ✕ ✓ ƒ×	139		
	A	B	C	D	E
1					
2			139		
3					

Entry being made

3 Press **[Enter]**. The cursor moves down to the cell below.

Enter values along a row

If you want to enter a series of values along a row, rather than down a column, complete the entry by pressing the right-arrow cursor key instead of **[Enter]**.

You can change the way Excel works so that pressing [Enter] moves the cursor to the right, rather than down. From the Tools menu, select Options, click on the Edit tab and make the appropriate selection in the 'Move selection after Enter' box. This change will affect all your worksheets.

Identify numeric and text entries

The position of the value in the cell depends on whether it is a number, a date or a piece of text:

- Numeric entries (starting with a + or - sign or a number, and containing only numeric characters) are placed on the right of the cell.

- Dates and times are also placed on the right. Excel interprets a variety of different formats as dates or times: e.g. 2/10/03, 2-10 and 5:15 (see page 80).

- Text entries (all other values) are placed on the left.

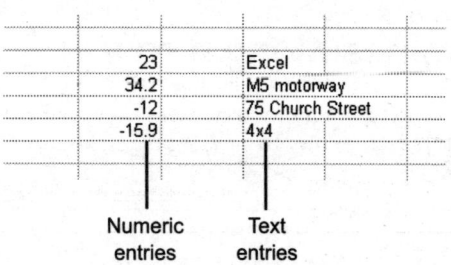

23	Excel
34.2	M5 motorway
-12	75 Church Street
-15.9	4x4

Numeric Text
entries entries

Values that start with +, - or = and contain other non-numeric characters (e.g. =B4+2) are assumed to be formulae: see page 119.

Enter a number as text

Sometimes you want to put a number in a cell but have Excel treat it as a piece of text: for example, if you are entering a year or a house number.

You can force Excel to treat the number as text by starting the entry with an apostrophe ('). The apostrophe is not displayed in the cell (but does appear in the formula bar when editing the cell).

A green triangle is shown in the cell corner. If you click on the cell, a warning symbol appears on the left. Place the pointer on the symbol to display a pop-up message or click for a menu of options.

Actual entry, shown in formula bar,
starts with an apostrophe

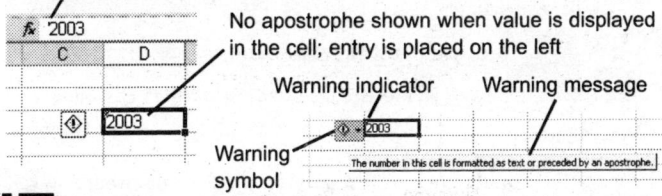

No apostrophe shown when value is displayed in the cell; entry is placed on the left

Warning indicator   Warning message

Warning
symbol

The number in this cell is formatted as text or preceded by an apostrophe.

tip

Start the entry with an apostrophe if the entry is a piece of text but begins with +, - or =. Start with two apostrophes if you want to display one apostrophe (e.g. a piece of text in single quotes). You may also need an apostrophe with dates: see page 80.

Replace an entry

To replace the entry in a cell with a new value:

1 Click on the cell.

2 Type the new value.

3 Press **[Enter]**.

Edit an entry

The quickest way to change an entry is often to replace it by typing a new value. However, you can also edit an existing value:

1 Click on the cell.

2 Click on the formula bar, where the value is now displayed.

3 Use the cursor keys, **[Delete]** and **[Backspace]** to edit the value.

4 Press **[Enter]**.

Alternatively, double-click on the cell to edit the value there.

tip

You can use the standard Windows cut-and-paste key combinations when editing the text in a cell. In the formula bar or cell, drag the pointer to mark a piece of text within the entry.

Abandon an entry

An incorrect entry can be cancelled either while it is still being typed or after it has been finished:

- If you are typing an entry in the wrong cell, press **[Esc]**. The entry is abandoned and any previous value is restored.

- If you have already pressed **[Enter]**, you can still remove the entry by pressing **[Ctrl]** and **[Z]** together. Your last action is cancelled and the previous contents of the cell are restored.

- If Excel detects an error in an entry it displays a warning message and gives you the chance to correct it. Pressing **[Esc]** abandons the entry altogether. Otherwise, you can make a correction to the entry and then press **[Enter]** to try again.

You can also cancel a series of your most recent actions. Excel provides options whereby you can view all the changes you made since the worksheet was last saved and then decide which of these are to be cancelled: see page 35.

Delete the contents of cells

To delete the contents of a single cell:

1 Click on the cell.

2 Press **[Delete]**.

To delete the contents of a range of cells:

1 Mark the range (see page 7).

2 Press **[Delete]**.

Don't try to delete the contents of a cell by blanking it out with the spacebar. Although the cell will look as if it is empty, the actual effect is that the cell contains a text entry made up of spaces. This may cause problems later on when you enter formulae that refer to the cell.

tip

If you delete a cell or range of cells accidentally, you can recover their contents by pressing [Ctrl] and [Z]. You can also undo a series of deletions, providing you have not saved the worksheet since making the changes: see page 35.

Copy a cell

The contents of a cell can be copied to another cell.

1 Click on the cell to be copied.

2 From the **Edit** menu, select **Copy**.

Or

Press **[Ctrl]** and **[C]** together.

3 The value is now held in the Windows clipboard. Click on the new cell and press **[Enter]**.

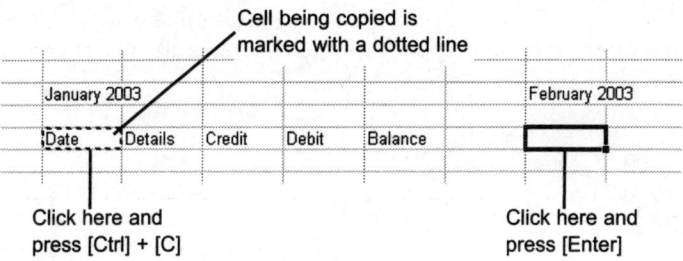

Cell being copied is marked with a dotted line

| January 2003 | | | | | February 2003 |
| Date | Details | Credit | Debit | Balance | |

Click here and press [Ctrl] + [C]

Click here and press [Enter]

tip

You can copy the contents of a cell to several cells or a marked range: see page 31.

Copy a range of cells

A range of cells can be copied to another location on the worksheet.

1 Mark the range to be copied.

2 From the **Edit** menu, select **Copy**.

Or

Press **[Ctrl]** and **[C]** together.

3 The range of values is now held in the Windows clipboard. Click on the cell that is to be the top left-hand corner of the new range and press **[Enter]**.

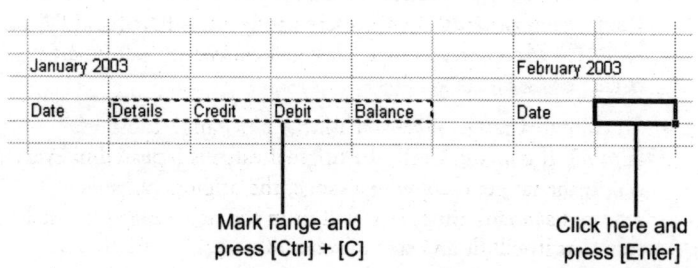

| January 2003 | | | | | | February 2003 | |
| Date | Details | Credit | Debit | Balance | | Date | |

Mark range and
press [Ctrl] + [C]

Click here and
press [Enter]

The values will be copied to this
cell and the three cells to the right

Make multiple copies

You can make copies of a cell or a range in several locations. Start by making a copy of the original cell or range.

1 Click on the cell or mark the range to be copied.

2 From the **Edit** menu, select **Copy**.

   Or

   Press **[Ctrl]** and **[C]** together.

The cell or range is held in the clipboard.

Now copy this data to the new locations:

- To copy to several locations, click on each cell in turn and select **Paste** from the **Edit** menu; alternatively, press **[Ctrl]** and **[V]** on each cell. If copying a range, each cell clicked is the top left-hand corner of a new range.

- To copy to a range of cells, mark the new range and press **[Enter]**. If copying a cell, the original value is repeated in every cell in the range; if copying a range, the original range is repeated as many times as it will fit in the new range (but make sure that it will fit an exact number of times).

Move a cell or range

The contents of a cell or range can be moved to another location.

1 Click on the cell or range to be moved.

2 From the **Edit** menu, select **Cut**.

   Or

   Press **[Ctrl]** and **[X]** together.

3 Click on the new cell (or the new top left-hand corner of the range) and press **[Enter]**.

The original cell or range is cleared and the values are moved to the new cell or range, replacing any existing values.

> After selecting Cut or Copy (so that the dotted border is displayed) you can cancel the action by pressing [Esc].

Repeat previous copies

Clipboard data is held in memory and can be copied to new locations later. The items that have been copied are listed on the Clipboard task pane, which is displayed when you copy several items.

You can paste any of the copied items into any location at any time:

1 Click on a cell.

2 Move the pointer over the Clipboard icons on the left of the task pane until you find the one you want.

3 Click on the icon.

You can turn off the task pane by clicking on its ✖ button.

tip

> The task pane can be switched on or off with Task Pane from the View menu. Use the down-arrow button to choose a different pane from the drop-down list.

Select different pane

Switch off task pane

Click on icon to copy its data

Data copied to the clipboard from another program

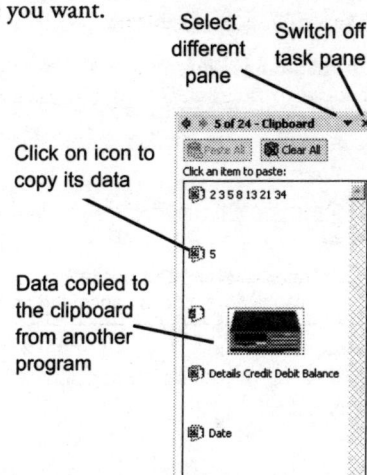

Fill a range with a series

Excel provides a simple way of filling a range with either the same item of data or a sequence of values.

To fill a range with a single value:

1 Type the value in the first cell.

2 Drag the 'fill handle' in the bottom right-hand corner of the cell over the column below or the row to the right.

The value is repeated in the marked cells.

To fill a range with a sequence of values:

1 Type the first and second values in the first two cells. Mark a range containing these cells.

2 Drag the 'fill handle' in the bottom right-hand corner of the cell over the column below or the row to the right.

In this case, the range is filled with a sequence of values, increasing or decreasing depending on the difference between the first two values.

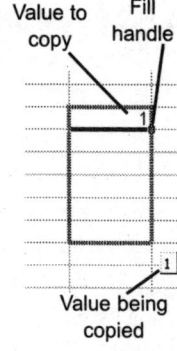

Value to copy   Fill handle

Value being copied

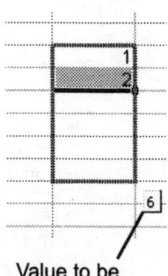

Value to be put in last cell

Cancel several actions

A series of the most recent actions can be cancelled in the following ways:

- Press **[Ctrl]** and **[Z]** for each of the actions to be cancelled. Alternatively, select **Undo** from the **Edit** menu.

- Click on the 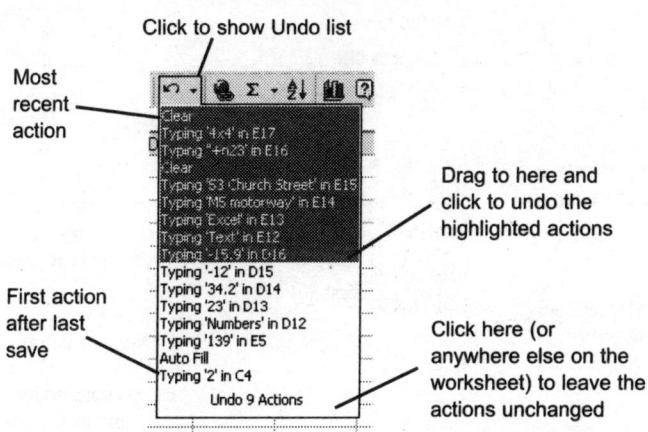 button the required number of times.

- Click on the arrow to the right of the button. The most recent actions are listed in reverse order. Drag the mouse to highlight those you want to cancel and click.

Click to show Undo list

Most recent action

Clear
Typing '4x4' in E17
Typing '+n23' in E16
Clear
Typing 'S3 Church Street' in E15
Typing 'M5 motorway' in E14
Typing 'Excel' in E13
Typing 'Text' in E12
Typing '15.9' in D16
Typing '-12' in D15
Typing '34.2' in D14
Typing '23' in D13
Typing 'Numbers' in D12
Typing '139' in E5
Auto Fill
Typing '2' in C4
Undo 9 Actions

Drag to here and click to undo the highlighted actions

First action after last save

Click here (or anywhere else on the worksheet) to leave the actions unchanged

Redo actions

If you have undone one or more actions by mistake you can restore them:

- Press **[Ctrl]** and **[Y]** for each action to be restored. Alternatively, select **Redo** from the **Edit** menu.

- Click on the ◌ button the required number of times.

- Click on the arrow to the right of the ◌ button. The actions that were undone are listed (in their original order). Drag the mouse to highlight those you want to restore and click.

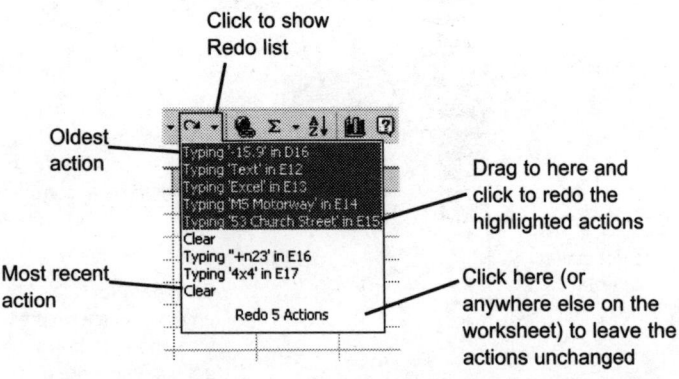

Click to show
Redo list

Oldest
action

Typing '15.9' in D16
Typing 'Text' in E12
Typing 'Excel' in E13
Typing 'M5 Motorway' in E14
Typing '53 Church Street' in E15
Clear
Typing "+n23" in E16
Typing '4x4' in E17
Clear

Redo 5 Actions

Most recent
action

Drag to here and
click to redo the
highlighted actions

Click here (or
anywhere else on the
worksheet) to leave the
actions unchanged

04

working with files

Save the file

The worksheet you have created should be saved in an Excel file.
You should save your file soon after you start.

1 From the **File** menu, select **Save**.

2 In the drop-down box at the top of the window, select the drive.

Create new
folder, if required

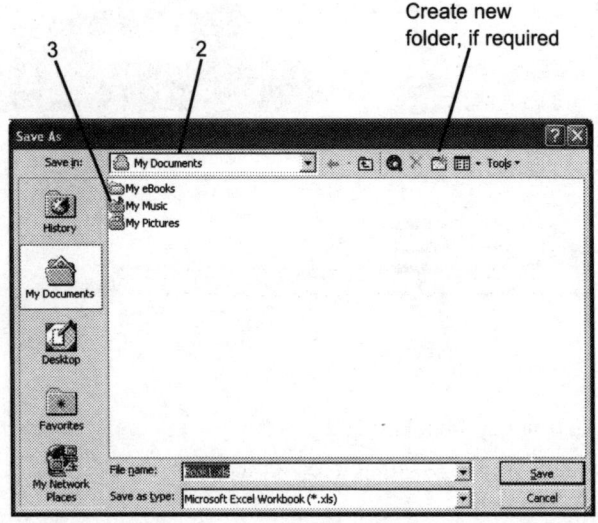

3 Open the directory where the file is to be stored, by double-clicking on the folder icons in the main part of the window.

4 Type a suitable name in the **File name** box.

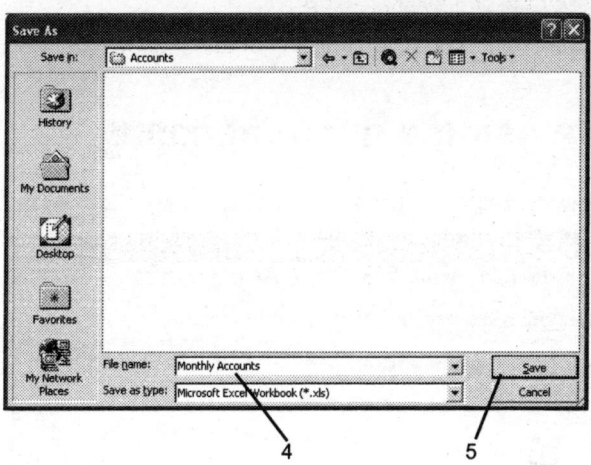

5 Click on the **Save** button.

Excel adds an 'xls' extension to the filename.

Resave a file

You should save the changes to your worksheet at regular intervals.

Either select **Save** from the **File** menu or click on the ■ button.

The current version of the worksheet replaces the existing worksheet.

Save using a different name

You may want to save a file using a different name; for example, you may want to keep an original version of a worksheet.

1 From the **File** menu, select **Save As**.

2 Select the directory and enter a new filename.

3 Click on the **Save** button.

The original file is unchanged, so you now have two versions of the file.

You can use this method to create a new file based on an existing one. Alternatively, you can create a template as the basis for new files (see page 43).

Store additional details

Excel allows you to store additional information for each file, such as the title of the file, the author's name and other, general comments.

1 From the **File** menu, select **Properties**. The Properties dialog is displayed, with the **Author** and **Company** names taken from the computer's registry entries.

2 Fill in the other boxes. You can use the boxes for any purpose you like. (You can also change the **Author** and **Company**, if necessary.)

3 Click on **OK**.

When you place the mouse pointer over an Excel filename in Windows Explorer, the author's name is shown in the pop-up label.

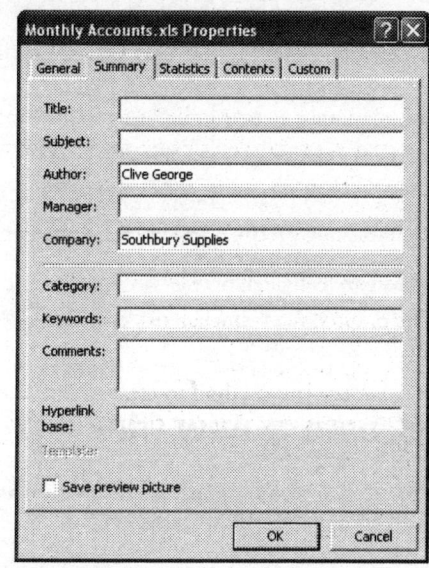

Monthly Accounts.xls Properties

General | Summary | Statistics | Contents | Custom

Title:

Subject:

Author: Clive George

Manager:

Company: Southbury Supplies

Category:

Keywords:

Comments:

Hyperlink base:

Template:

☐ Save preview picture

OK | Cancel

Load a file

To load an existing worksheet:

1 From the **File** menu, select **Open**.

2 In the box at
the top of the
dialog, find the
directory where
the file is stored.

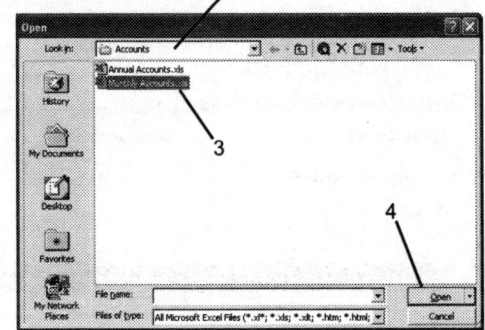

3 Click on the
file, which will
have an 'xls'
extension.

4 Click on **Open**.

Alternatively: click on the 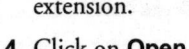 icon on the toolbar; click on a
recently-used file at the bottom of the **File** menu; or select a file
from the task pane.

Create a new file

To create a new file, click on the ⬜ icon on the toolbar. The file
will contain a blank worksheet.

Create a template

If you create similar worksheets on a regular basis (e.g. monthly reports, invoices), you can save a basic worksheet as a template.

1 From the **File** menu, select **Save As**.

2 In the **Save as type** box, select **Template (*.xlt)**.

3 If necessary, change the filename. Excel will add an 'xlt' extension.

4 Click on **Save**.

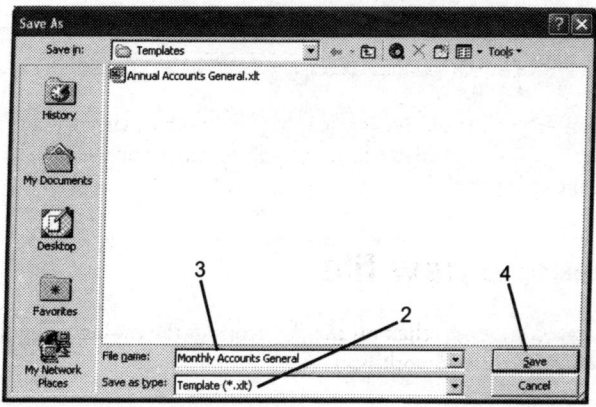

Use a template

To create a file based on a template:

1 From the **File** menu, select **New**.

2 Select the required template from the task pane.

3 Click on **OK**.

Use an existing file
as the basis for the
new file (the existing
file is not changed)

Select a template
as the basis for
the new file

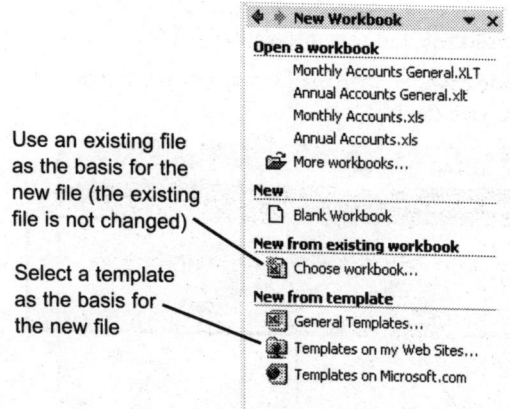

4 Use **Save As** from the **File** menu to save the file as an 'xls' file.
The template file is unchanged.

Close a file

When you have finished working with a worksheet, close the file.

1 From the **File** menu, select **Close**.

   Or

   Click on the 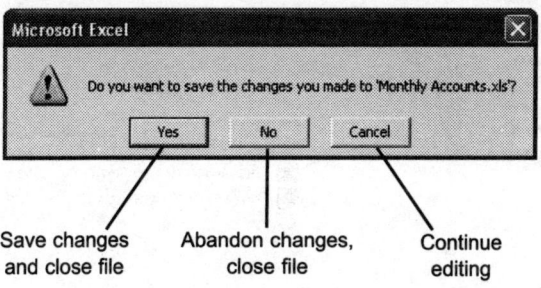 button in the worksheet window.

   Or

   Click on the worksheet and then press **[Ctrl] + [W]**.

2 If you have made changes since the file was last saved, you will be prompted to save the file.

Microsoft Excel	⊠
⚠ Do you want to save the changes you made to 'Monthly Accounts.xls'?	
Yes No Cancel	

Save changes   Abandon changes,   Continue
and close file   close file   editing

05
worksheet layout

Change the default column width

The width of the columns in a worksheet is given in terms of the average number of characters (in the standard Windows font) that will fit in a column. By default, the width is 8.43 characters.

To change the default width for all columns in the worksheet:

1 From the **Format** menu, select **Column** and **Standard Width**.

2 Type a new value in the dialog box.

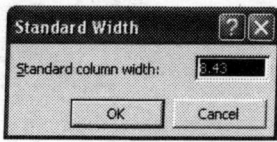

3 Click on **OK**.

If a column is not wide enough to display a large numeric value, the cell is filled with # characters. Even though you cannot see the number, it is still held in memory. When you increase the column width, the number is displayed.

Change the width of specific columns

To change the width of one or more columns:

1 Click on a cell or mark a range that covers a number of columns.

2 From the **Format** menu, select **Column** and **Width**.

3 Enter the new width for the selected columns.

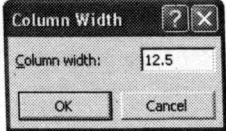

4 Click on **OK**.

Or

If the precise width is not important, drag the border on the right of the column letter (at the top of the worksheet) until the column is the required width.

Drag here, to right or left, to change the width of column A

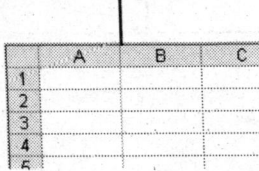

To mark several complete columns, click on the first column letter, hold down [Shift], then click on the last column letter.

Make column widths fit text

If you type an item of text that is wider than the column, the text will spill over to the next column (providing the adjacent cell is empty). You can make the column width match the width of the text.

1 Click on a cell with wide text or mark a range of cells.

2 From the **Format** menu, select **Column** and **AutoFit Selection**.

Or

Double-click on the border on the right of the column letter (at the top of the worksheet).

Double-click here to
change the width of
column C to match the
longest item of text in
the column

Column width increased to
allow for wide text

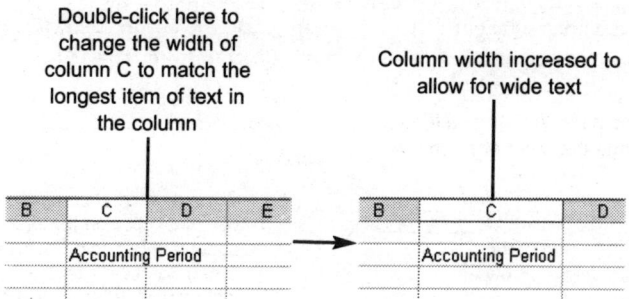

Change the height of rows

The height of rows is given in terms of points. There are 72 points to the inch; the standard Windows font uses 10-point characters. By default, the row height is 12.75 points.

To change the height of one or more rows:

1 Click on a cell or mark a range that covers a number of rows.

2 From the **Format** menu, select **Row** and **Height**.

3 Enter the new height
for the selected rows.

4 Click on **OK**.

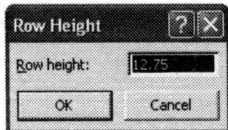

Or

If the precise height is not important, drag the border below the row number (on the left of the worksheet) until the row is the required height.

Drag here, up
or down, to
change the
height of row 2

Make row heights fit the text

If you change the font size for the text in a row, the height of the row changes to fit the new font (see page 88). If you subsequently change the row height, you can make the row fit the text again as follows:

1 Click on a cell in the row or mark a range of cells.

2 From the **Format** menu, select **Row** and **AutoFit**.

Or

Double-click on the border below the row number (on the left of the worksheet).

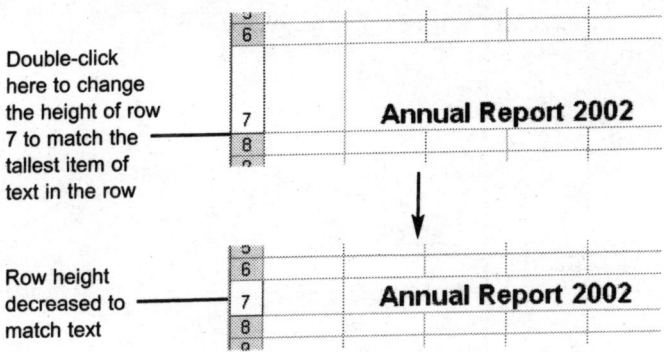

Double-click here to change the height of row 7 to match the tallest item of text in the row

Annual Report 2002

Row height decreased to match text

Annual Report 2002

Wrap text within a cell

If there is more text than will fit in one cell but you do not want it to spread onto neighbouring cells, you can make it wrap over onto a number of lines within the cell.

1 Click on the cell.

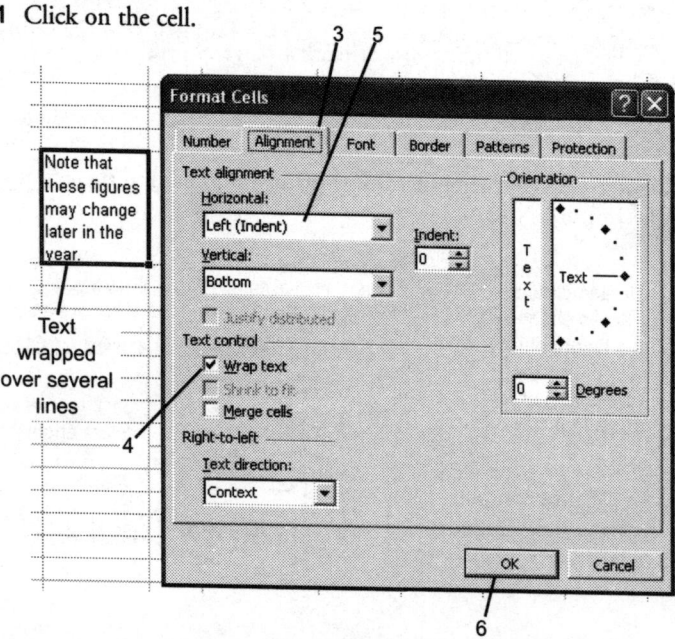

Note that these figures may change later in the year.

Text wrapped over several lines

2 From the **Format** menu, select **Cells**.

3 Click on the **Alignment** tab.

4 Click on the **Wrap text** check box.

5 In the **Horizontal** box, choose **Left**, **Center**, **Right** or **Justify** to set the position of the text within the cell. (Justified text is padded with extra space so that it reaches both edges of the cell.)

6 Click on **OK**.

The row containing the wrapped text expands to display the whole of the text.

> By default, all text is displayed at the bottom of the cell. You can show the text (whether or not it is wrapped) in the centre or top of the cell by selecting the relevant option from the Vertical box in the Alignment tab.

You can change the angle of text in the cell by clicking on a marker in the **Orientation** box or entering the required angle in degrees.

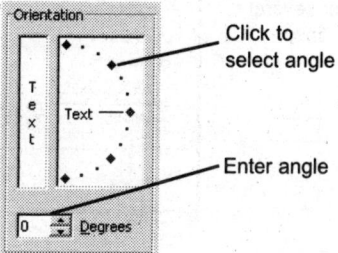

Click to select angle

Enter angle

Change text alignment

When you start a worksheet, text is displayed on the left of the cell and numbers are placed on the right. You can change the alignment of a cell or range:

1 Click on the cell or mark the range.

2 Click on the appropriate button on the Alignment toolbar.

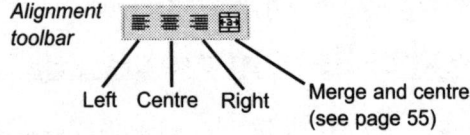

Alignment toolbar

Left   Centre   Right   Merge and centre (see page 55)

Or

Select **Cells** from the **Format** menu, click on the **Alignment** tab and choose the required option in the **Horizontal** box.

Day:	Monday		OPTIONS
Date:	14/05/2003		Add
Time:	14:20		Edit
			Delete
Ref. No:	3204		Next

Right   Left
aligned   aligned   Centred

Centre text over a range

Wide items of text, such as headings, may need to be centred over a range of cells. There are two ways of centring text:

- Merge a range of cells and centre the combined text across the range.
- Centre one item of text across a range but leave the underlying cells unchanged.

Merge cells and centre text

To merge a range of cells and centre the text within them:

1 Mark the range that is to be covered by the text.

2 Click on the 田 button.

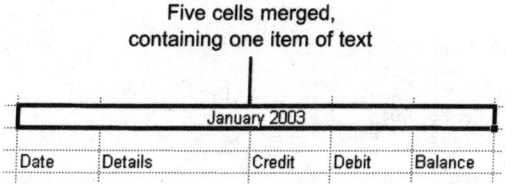

Five cells merged, containing one item of text

January 2003				
Date	Details	Credit	Debit	Balance

Centre text without merging

To centre text without merging the cells:

1 Mark the range that is to be covered by the text. Only one cell should contain text; the others must be empty.

2 From the **Format** menu, select **Cells**.

3 Click on the **Alignment** tab.

4 Click on the **Horizontal** box and choose **Center Across Selection**.

5 Check that the **Merge cells** box is not ticked.

6 Click on **OK**.

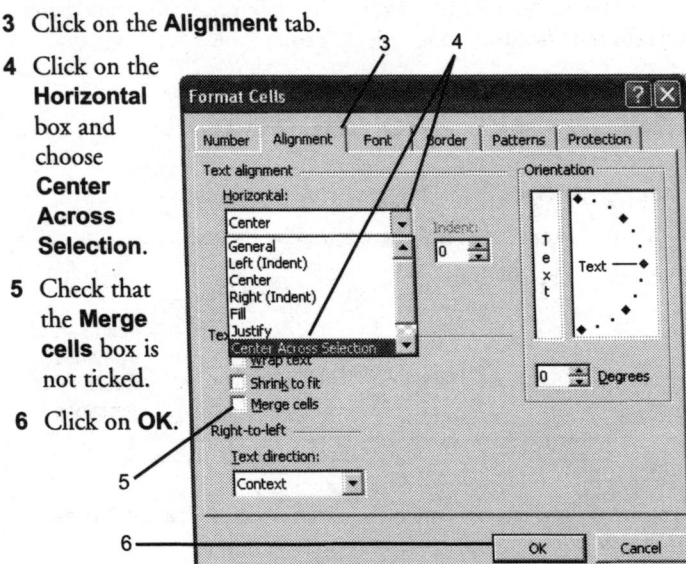

Freeze rows and columns

In large worksheets, there are often columns on the left of the sheet or rows at the top which you want to be able to see all the time. Excel allows you to fix these areas so that they are always visible.

1 Click on the cell that is to be the top left-hand corner of the free-moving area of the sheet.

2 From the **Window** menu, select **Freeze Panes**.

The screen is now divided into four areas.

Top left-hand corner
completely fixed

	A	F	G	
1				
2		Position Information		Top rows scroll left
3				and right
4	Payroll No.	Department	Position No.	
21	25906	Finance	D345	
22	25975	Sales	W75	Main part of
23	26034	Sales	D356	worksheet
24	26338	Finance	N8	scrolls in all
25	26870	Production	E47	directions
26	27809	Sales	D355	
27				

Left-hand columns scroll up and down

To restore normal movement in the sheet, select **Unfreeze Panes** from the **Window** menu.

Hide rows or columns

You may want to hide particular rows or columns for a number of reasons (for example, to hide the intermediate stages in a complicated calculation).

1 Click on a cell or mark a range covering the rows or columns to be hidden.

2 From the **Format** menu, select either **Row** or **Column**, then select **Hide**.

The rows or columns disappear from view but the contents of their cells are unaffected. There will be a gap in the row numbers or column letters and the dividing line in the row or column border is slightly thicker.

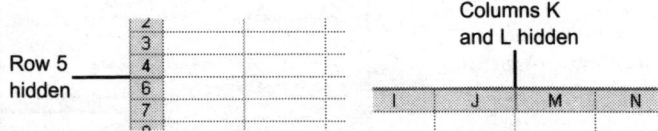

Row 5 hidden

Columns K and L hidden

To show the rows or columns again:

1 Mark a range covering cells on both sides of the hidden rows or columns.

2 From the **Format** menu, select either **Row** or **Column**, then click on **Unhide**.

Insert rows or columns

To insert a single row or column:

1 Right-click on a row number or column letter.

2 The row or column is highlighted and a menu is displayed. Click on **Insert**.

New rows are inserted above the highlighted row but have the same format as the row above the new row; columns are inserted to the left of the highlighted column but have the same format as the column to the left.

To insert several rows or columns:

1 Drag the mouse pointer across the required number of row numbers or column labels and right-click.

2 The rows or columns are highlighted and a menu is displayed. Click on **Insert**.

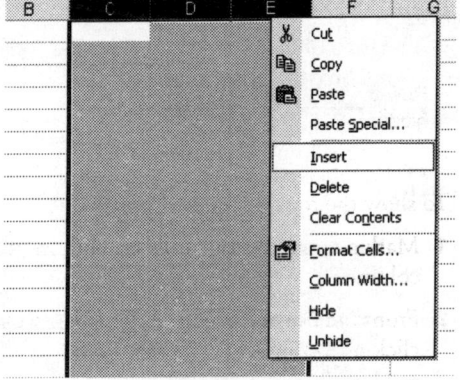

Delete rows or columns

To delete a single row or column:

1 Right-click on the row number or column letter.

2 The row or column is highlighted and a menu is displayed. Click on **Delete**.

The row or column is deleted and the remaining rows below or columns to the right are relabelled.

To delete several rows or columns:

1 Drag the mouse pointer across the relevant row numbers or column labels and right-click.

2 The rows or columns are highlighted and a menu is displayed. Click on **Delete**.

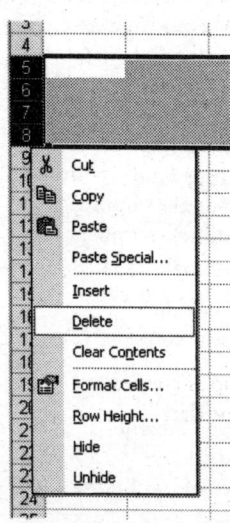

When you hide rows or columns, the data is still held in the worksheet even though it is not visible (see page 58); when you delete rows or columns, the data is lost.

Insert cells

You can insert a range of cells, moving the contents of all cells to the right of or below the range to make room for the new range.

1 Mark the area where you want to insert the cells.

2 Right-click and select **Insert**.

3 Click on **Shift cells right** to move the contents of the marked range (and all cells to the right of the range) further to the right.

Alternatively, click on **Shift cells down** to move the range (and the cells below) down.

03/06/2000	8 12/14	11 6/14	2 8/14
08/07/2000	8 12/14	11 3/14	
09/08/2000	8 13/14	11 5/14	
07/09/2000	8 12/14	11 4/14	
04/10/2000	8 13/14	11 6/14	
02/11/2000	9 4/14	11 10/14	
07/12/2000	9	11 6/14	
06/01/2001	9 2/14	11 5/14	
06/02/2001	9 2/14	11 3/14	
02/03/2001			
01/04/2001			

Insert ? X

Insert
○ Shift cells right
● Shift cells down
○ Entire row
○ Entire column

OK   Cancel

4 Click on **OK**.

A gap is created in the data.

08/07/2000	8 12/14	11 3/14	2 5/14
09/08/2000	8 13/14	11 5/14	2 6/14
07/09/2000	8 12/14	11 4/14	2 6/14
04/10/2000	8 13/14	11 6/14	2 7/14
02/11/2000			2 6/14
07/12/2000			2 6/14
06/01/2001	9 4/14	11 10/14	2 3/14
06/02/2001	9	11 6/14	2 1/14
02/03/2001	9 2/14	11 5/14	0
01/04/2001	9 2/14	11 3/14	0

Delete cells

You can delete a range of cells, filling the gap with the contents of all cells to the right of or below the range.

1 Mark the range to be deleted.

2 Right-click and select **Delete**.

3 Click on **Shift cells left** or **Shift cells up**, depending on how you want to fill the gap.

4 Click on **OK**.

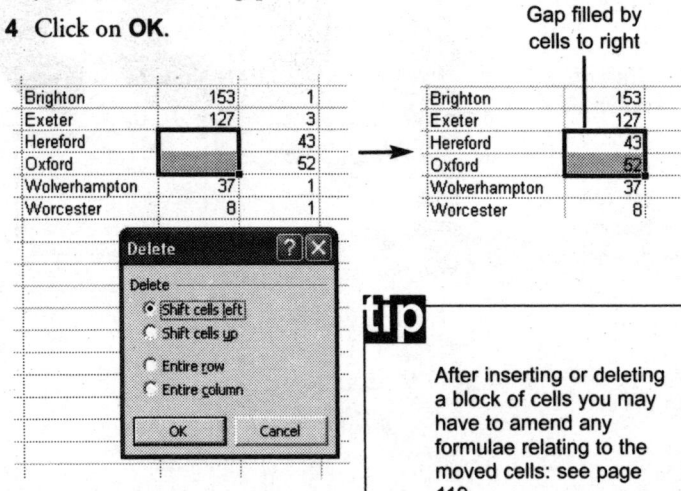

Gap filled by cells to right

Brighton	153	1
Exeter	127	3
Hereford		43
Oxford		52
Wolverhampton	37	1
Worcester	8	1

Brighton	153	
Exeter	127	
Hereford	43	
Oxford	52	
Wolverhampton	37	
Worcester	8	

Delete ? X

Delete
- ● Shift cells left
- ○ Shift cells up
- ○ Entire row
- ○ Entire column

OK   Cancel

tip

After inserting or deleting a block of cells you may have to amend any formulae relating to the moved cells: see page 119.

06

number formats

Use the General format

You can choose the format for displaying values for each individual cell. For instance, you may want to display numbers with two decimal places or show negative values in a different colour.

By default, all cells in a new worksheet are given the General format. With this format, the numeric contents of each cell are displayed using the most appropriate style:

- Whole numbers are displayed with no decimal places.

- Very large or very small numbers are shown using Scientific notation (see page 74).

- Other numeric values are displayed with as many decimal places as are necessary.

- Dates and times are displayed in the most appropriate date/time format.

To apply a different format when displaying numbers:

1 Click on the cell or mark the range to which the format is to apply.

2 From the **Format** menu, select **Cells**.

Or

Right-click on the cell or range and select **Format Cells**.

3 If necessary, click on the **Number** tab.

4 Click on a **Category**.

5 Select from the other options (which vary for each category): e.g. number of decimal places.

6 Click on **OK**.

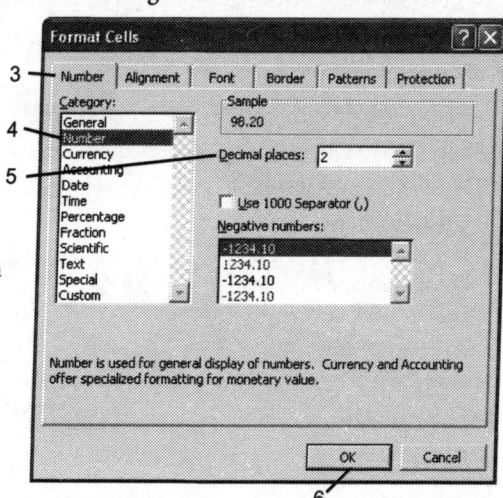

Apply the Number format

The confusingly-named Number format displays values with a fixed number of decimal places and has a range of options for the display of negative numbers. Values with fewer decimal places than specified are padded with zeros on the right; those with too many decimal places are rounded to the nearest appropriate value (e.g. for two decimal places, 98.207 and 98.212 are both shown as 98.21).

1 From the **Format** menu, select **Cells** and click on the **Number** tab.

2 From the **Category** box, select **Number**.

3 Set the number of decimal places to be shown.

4 Specify whether you want to use commas to separate each block of three digits for numbers over 1000.

5 Choose a format for negative numbers. The options include the use of red or black text and whether or not the minus sign is shown.

6 Click on **OK**.

tip

To round values to the nearest whole number, set the number of decimal places to 0.

Apply the Currency format

The Currency format inserts a monetary symbol (e.g. £) in the display and shows values with a fixed number of decimal places.

1 From the **Format** menu, select **Cells** and click on the **Number** tab.

2 From the **Category** box, select **Currency**.

3 Set the number of decimal places to be shown.

4 Click on the **Symbol** box to choose a currency symbol from the drop-down list.

5 Choose a format for negative numbers.

6 Click on **OK**.

tip

Don't type a currency symbol when entering a value, as the entry will be treated as text. Apply the Currency format instead.

Exchange rate		
€/£	£	€
1.5699	£0.01	€ 0.02
	£0.10	€ 0.16
	£0.50	€ 0.78
	£1.00	€ 1.57
	£5.00	€ 7.85
	£10.00	€ 15.70
	£50.00	€ 78.50
	£100.00	€ 156.99

£ symbols added automatically

Apply the Accounting format

The Accounting format is similar to the Currency format but all currency symbols are lined up on the left of the cell. Negative numbers have a minus sign to the left of the currency symbol.

1 From the **Format** menu, select **Cells** and click on the **Number** tab.

2 From the **Category** box, select **Accounting**.

3 Set the number of decimal places to be shown.

4 Click on the **Symbol** box to choose a currency symbol from the drop-down list.

5 Click on **OK**.

Exchange rate				
€/£		£		€
1.5699	£	0.01	€	0.02
	£	0.10	€	0.16
	£	0.50	€	0.78
	£	1.00	€	1.57
	£	5.00	€	7.85
	£	10.00	€	15.70
	£	50.00	€	78.50
	£	100.00	€	156.99

£ symbols displayed on left

Apply the Percentage format

The Percentage format presents the value in a cell as a percentage of the entered or calculated number (e.g. an entry of 0.333 is shown as 33.3%).

1 From the **Format** menu, select **Cells** and click on the **Number** tab.

2 From the **Category** box, select **Percentage**.

3 Set the number of decimal places to be shown. (This is the number of decimal places of one per cent: for example, one decimal place for a display of 33.3%.)

4 Click on **OK**.

tip

If you type a percentage symbol when entering a value in a General-format cell, the cell is converted to Percentage format for you. If the percentage symbol was typed by mistake, you will have to remove the cell formatting (see page 71).

Apply the Fraction format

The Fraction format displays values as fractions, rather than decimals. This is useful for entering values that do not convert easily into decimals: for example, times in hours and minutes or weights in pounds and ounces.

1 From the **Format** menu, select **Cells** and click on the **Number** tab.

2 From the **Category** box, select **Fraction**.

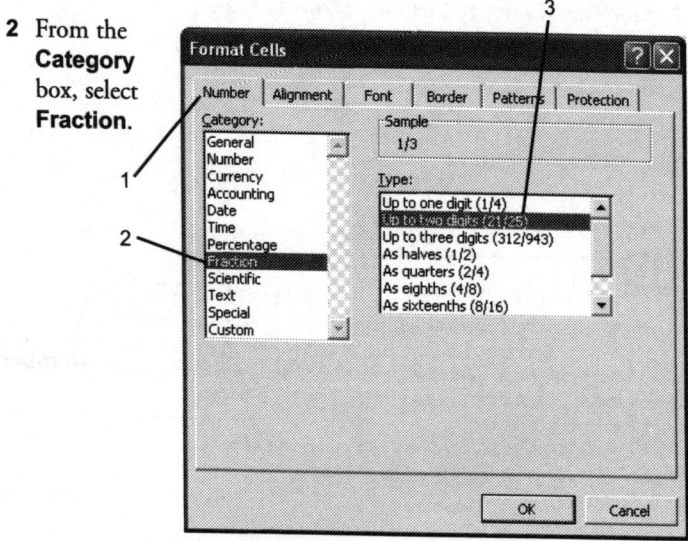

3 Choose the type of fraction you want to display. You can set the number to be displayed on the bottom of the fraction or specify the maximum number of digits.

4 Click on **OK**.

When cells have been given the Fraction format you can enter values as fractions, with a space between the whole number and the fraction (e.g. '2 7/60').

0.1	10.00%	1/10
0.25	25.00%	1/4
0.3333	33.33%	1/3
0.81	81.00%	64/79
0.9999	99.99%	1

General   Percentage   Fraction

Remove formats

You can remove the number formatting from a cell by re-applying the General format.

1 From the **Format** menu, select **Cells** and click on the **Number** tab.

2 From the **Category** box, select **General**.

3 Click on **OK**.

Convert stored values to displayed precision

Numbers are held in memory with an accuracy of up to 15 significant figures, even though they may be displayed with less precision.

When the number of decimal places has to be reduced for a particular format, the entry is rounded to the nearest value with that number of decimal places. For example, to display whole numbers, values where the decimal part is greater than or equal to 0.5 are rounded up to the nearest whole number; those less than 0.5 are rounded down. So 3.3, 3.49 and 3.49995 are rounded down to 3 while 3.7, 3.5001 and 3.5 are rounded up to 4.

X	Y	
3.3	5.4	——— General format
3	5	——— Number format, 0 decimal places

Similarly, for 2 decimal places, 3.354 is rounded down to 3.35 while 3.355 rounds up to 3.36.

Calculations that refer to these cells use the stored values rather than the displayed numbers, sometimes appearing to give incorrect results.

X	Y	X + Y	
3.3	5.4	8.7	—— General format
3	5	9	—— Number format, 0 decimal places

You can change the way Excel works, so that the values in memory match those displayed. This is useful when dealing with money values, for instance, where you want the results of calculations to be a precise amount (e.g. 17.5% of £18.30 should be £3.20, not £3.2025).

1 From the **Tools** menu, select **Options**.

2 Click on the **Calculation** tab.

3 Click on **Precision as displayed**.

4 Click on **OK**.

Note that this setting applies to the whole file, not just the current range.

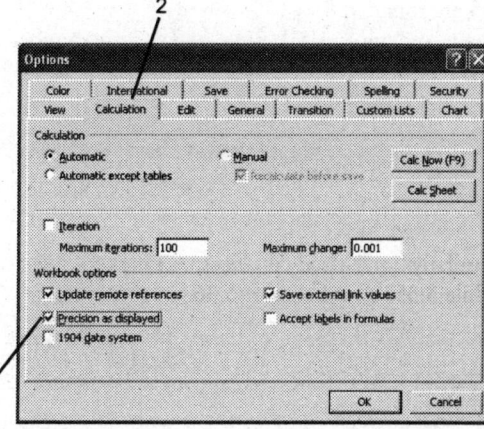

Use the Scientific format

If a calculation results in a very large or very small number, Excel displays the result in Scientific notation.

X	0.0243
Y	1000000
X / Y	2.43E-08

Scientific notation:
$2.43E-08 = 2.43 \times 10^{-8}$
$= 2.43 / 100000000$
$= 0.0000000243$

The number is interpreted as follows:

- The value to the left of 'E' is in the range 1 to 9.99.

- The value to the right of 'E' is a power of 10.

- The number represented by the cell is found by multiplying the left-hand side by 10 to the power of the value on the right.

For example:

$2.43E+02 = 2.43 \times 10^2 = 2.43 \times 100 = 243$
$2.43E+08 = 2.43 \times 10^8 = 2.43 \times 100000000 = 243000000$
$2.43E+00 = 2.43 \times 10^0 = 2.43 \times 1 = 2.43$
$2.43E-02 = 2.43 / 10^2 = 2.43 / 100 = 0.0243$
$2.43E-08 = 2.43 / 10^8 = 2.43 / 100000000 = 0.0000000243$

Scientific format displays all numbers in Scientific notation, regardless of their size. To change a normal value to Scientific format:

1 From the **Format** menu, select **Cells** and click on the **Number** tab.

2 From the **Category** box, select **Scientific**.

3 Set the number of decimal places to be shown. (This is the number of decimal places for the value on the left of 'E'.)

4 Click on **OK**.

Note the following:

- Multiplying by 10 adds 1 to the value on the right of the 'E'; dividing by 10 subtracts 1.

- When two Scientific-format numbers are multiplied, the values on the left of 'E' are multiplied and those on the right are added. For division, the values on the left are divided and those on the right are subtracted.

If General format cells are shown in Scientific format, you can force the display to be in decimals by changing to the Number format.

Design a custom format

If none of the predefined number formats is quite right, you can design your own.

1 From the **Format** menu, select **Cells** and click on the **Number** tab.

2 From the **Category** box, select **Custom**.

3 Click on a format in the **Type** list that is close to what you want.

4 In the **Type** box at the top of the list, amend the format using the codes below.

5 Click on **OK**.

The format has four sections, one for each of the following types of value:

- Positive numbers
- Negative numbers
- Zero
- Non-numeric values

The four sections are separated by semi-colons (;). If sections are omitted, the format defaults to an appropriate Number format for any corresponding values.

Each section is made up of the following characters:

- # or 0 for each digit; use 0 if you want zeros to be printed even when they are at the front or back of the number.

- ? after the decimal point to display a space for a zero at the end of the number (so values line up at the decimal point).

- Decimal point (.).

- Comma (,) if the thousands separator is to be used.

- Minus sign (-) or brackets for negative numbers.

- Symbols such as £, $ and % to be added to the display.

- The @ symbol if text is to be displayed as entered.

- Additional text in double quotes (" ").

- Colours in square brackets.

Use a custom format

To apply your own format:

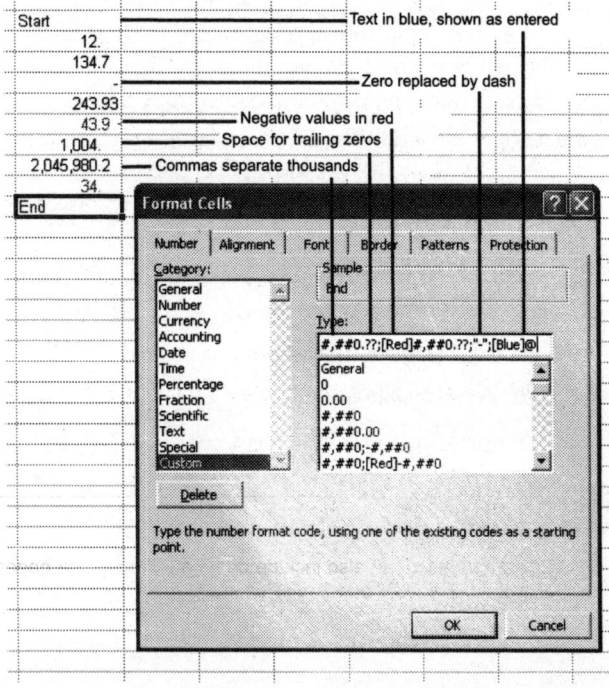

Start   — Text in blue, shown as entered

12.

134.7   — Zero replaced by dash

243.93

43.9   — Negative values in red

1,004.   — Space for trailing zeros

2,045,980.2   — Commas separate thousands

34.

End

Format Cells

Number | Alignment | Font | Border | Patterns | Protection

Category:

General
Number
Currency
Accounting
Date
Time
Percentage
Fraction
Scientific
Text
Special
Custom

Sample

End

Type:

#,##0.??;[Red]#,##0.??;"-";[Blue]@

General
0
0.00
#,##0
#,##0.00
#,##0;-#,##0
#,##0;[Red]-#,##0

Delete

Type the number format code, using one of the existing codes as a starting point.

OK   Cancel

1 From the **Format** menu, select **Cells** and click on the **Number** tab.

2 From the **Category** box, select **Custom**.

3 Click on your format in the **Type** list.

4 Click on **OK**.

In the example opposite, the four sections are as follows:

#,##0.??   Positive numbers have comma separators; one digit always shown to left of decimal point; two decimal places; missing decimals replaced by spaces.

[Red]#,##0.??   Negative numbers shown in red; otherwise, as for positive numbers.

-   Zero shown as dash.

[Blue]@   Text displayed in blue; shown as entered.

Custom formats can also include dates and times; see pages 80 and 82 for the Date and Time formats.

Display dates

If you enter a value that could be interpreted as a date, Excel displays it in one of the Date formats. For example, an entry of '1-5' or '1/5' is converted to the date '01-May', while '1-5-3' displays as '01/05/2003'. (In fact, Excel converts the cells to Custom format, selecting the most appropriate date style within that format.)

To display a date so that the month is shown as text:

1 From the **Format** menu, select **Cells** and click on the **Number** tab.

2 From the **Category** box, select **Date**.

3 If necessary, select a different country from the **Locale** box.

4 Select a style from the **Type** list to give the required format (e.g. '1-May-2003' or 'May 1, 2003').

5 Click on **OK**.

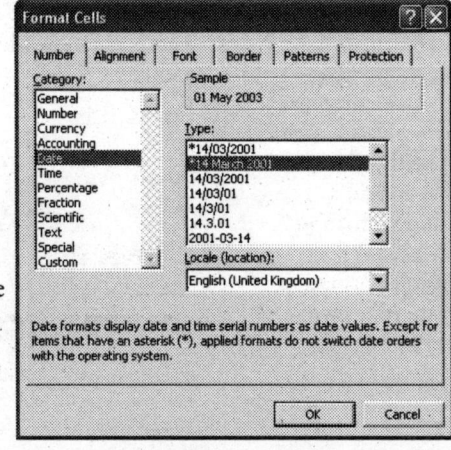

The predefined dates also include styles that show the month as a number but these all put the month before the day.

To display a date so that the month is shown as a number and comes after the day:

1 From the **Format** menu, select **Cells** and click on the **Number** tab.

2 From the **Category** box, select **Custom**.

3 Select a style from the **Type** list to give the required format (e.g. 'dd/mm/yyyy').

4 Click on **OK**.

Note that when the day is less than 10, the Date formats show a single digit while the Custom formats add a leading zero. You can amend the Custom formats or create your own format (see page 76).

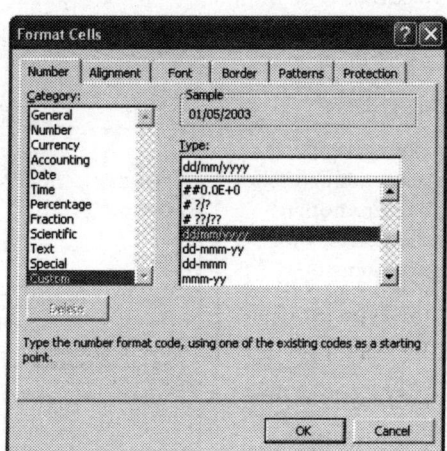

Display times

As for dates, Excel recognizes certain entries as times (e.g. '3:15' displays as '03:15'). To change the way a time is displayed:

1 From the **Format** menu, select **Cells** and click on the **Number** tab.

2 From the **Category** box, select either **Time** or **Custom**.

3 If necessary, select a different country from the **Locale** box.

4 Select a style from the **Type** list to give the required format. Various combinations of hours, minutes, seconds and tenths of seconds are available, with options for displaying the 24-hour clock or adding 'AM' and 'PM' to the time.

5 Click on **OK**.

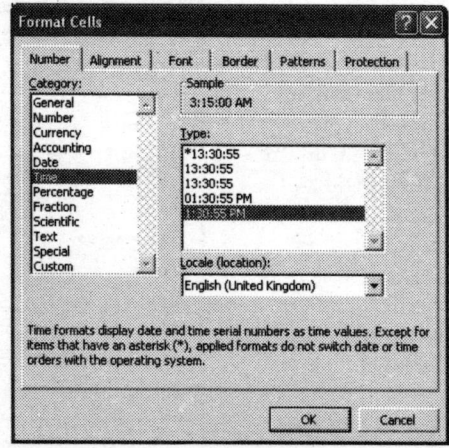

Display dates and times together

If you type a piece of text that includes both a date and time, Excel converts the cell to the appropriate format. You can change this to another date/time format.

1 From the **Format** menu, select **Cells** and click on the **Number** tab.

2 From the **Category** box, select **Date**, **Time** or **Custom**.

3 For the Date or Time categories, change the **Locale** if necessary.

4 Select a style from the **Type** list to give the required combined format.

5 Click on **OK**.

You can amend any of the Custom formats or design your own (see page 76).

If a cell contains a combined date and time you can change to a format where only the date or time is shown. However, the full date and time are still held in memory and will be displayed when you select one of the combined Date or Time formats. See page 84 for information on how dates and times are stored.

Convert date and time displays to numbers

Dates and times are actually stored as numbers rather than text:

- Dates are held as the number of days since 30/12/1899 (e.g. an entry of '1-5-01' is displayed as '01/05/2001' but held in memory as 37012).

- Times are held as a number representing the proportion of the day, giving values between 0 and 1 (e.g. '03:15' is held as 0.135417).

- Combined dates and times combine the two values (e.g. '01/05/2001 03:15' is held as 37012.135417).

You can show the number representing a date or time by changing the format:

1 Click on the cell or mark the range containing the dates/times.

2 From the **Format** menu, select **Cells** and click on the **Number** tab.

3 From the **Category** box, select either **General** or **Number**.

4 Click on **OK**.

Convert numbers to dates and times

You can convert any number to its equivalent date or time.

1 Click on the cell or mark the range containing the numbers.

2 From the **Format** menu, select **Cells** and click on the **Number** tab.

3 From the **Category** box, select **Date**, **Time** or **Custom**.

4 Choose a style from the **Type** list.

5 Click on **OK**.

Number	Date/Time
36951	01/03/2001	——— Custom format (dd/mm/yyyy)
0.75	18:00	——— Custom format (hh:mm)
36951.75	01/03/2001 18:00	——— Custom format (dd/mm/yyyy hh:mm)

General
format

07

worksheet cosmetics

Use a picture as the sheet background

To display a picture behind the worksheet:

1 From the **Format** menu, select **Sheet** and **Background**.
2 Find the directory containing the required picture.
3 Click on the picture file.
4 Click on **Insert**.

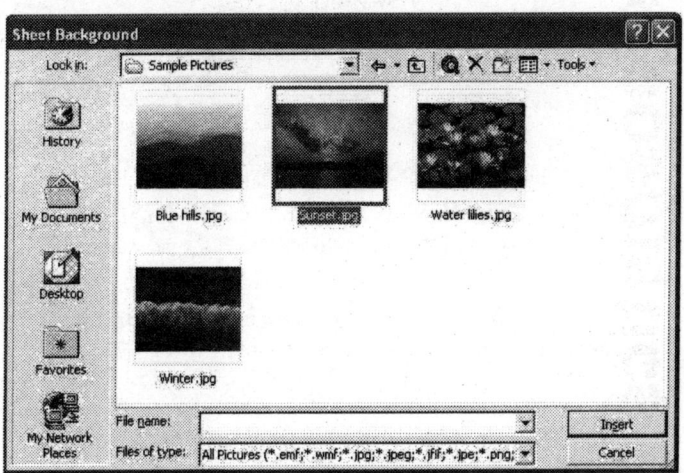

Change the font for a cell

By default, all cells in the worksheet display text and numbers in the 10-point Arial font.

To change the font, select the cell or range to which the changes are to apply and then use the font boxes and buttons on the toolbar.

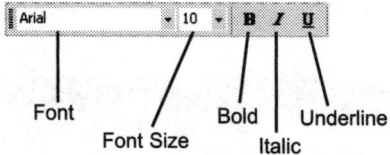

Font

Font Size

Bold

Italic

Underline

- Click on the **Font** box to select a new typeface from the list.

- Click on the **Font Size** box to select a new size (in points). Alternatively, type a value in the box. You can type values not included in the list (e.g. 7.5 point).

- Click on the **Bold**, **Italic** or **Underline** buttons to turn those attributes on. Click again to turn them off.

14-point, bold

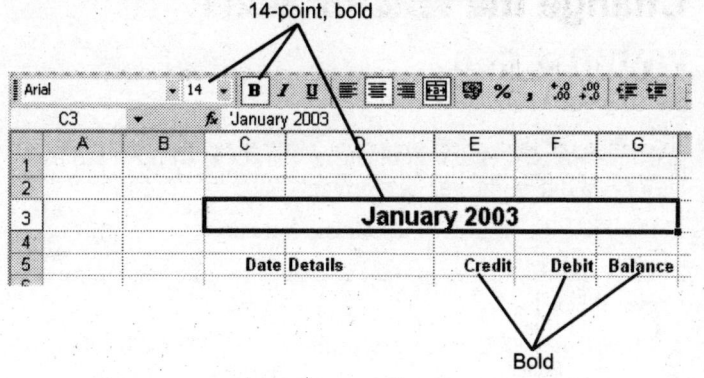

Bold

16-point, bold

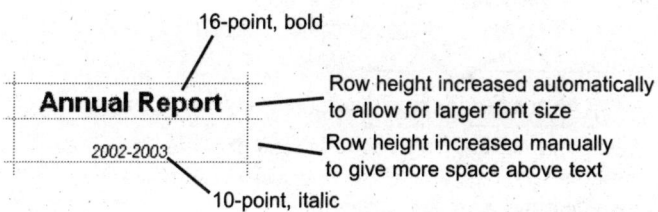

Annual Report — Row height increased automatically to allow for larger font size

— Row height increased manually to give more space above text

2002-2003

10-point, italic

When you increase the font size, the row height increases automatically; if you decrease the font size, the row height decreases.

Change the font for text within a cell

You can change the font for just some of the characters in a cell that contains text. (You cannot change part of a cell if the cell has been given one of the number formats.)

1 Double-click on the cell to edit the contents.

2 Mark the characters you want to change by dragging the cursor over them.

3 Change the typeface, size and attributes using the toolbar buttons.

Single character   Mark character by
set to 24-point   dragging cursor

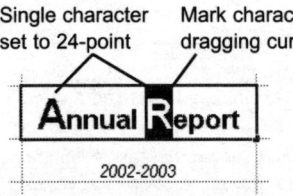

2002-2003

You can also use the following shortcut keys:

[Ctrl] + [B]   Bold

[Ctrl] + [I]   Italic

[Ctrl] + [U]   Underline

> You can change the font using the Font tab in the Format Cells dialog. This tab also includes an option that allows the Strikethrough effect to be applied to the text.

Display superscript and subscript text

To include superscript or subscript characters in a cell:

1 Double-click on a cell.

2 Mark the characters.

3 From the **Format** menu, select **Cells**. If the whole cell has been selected, click on the **Font** tab.

4 Click on the **Superscript** or **Subscript** check box to select it. Only one of these boxes can be selected at a time.

5 Click on **OK**.

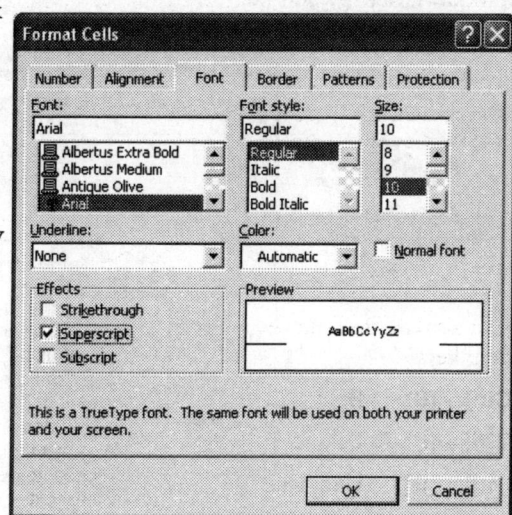

Change the text colour for a cell

To change the colour of the contents (text or numbers) of one or
more cells:

1 Select a cell or mark a range.

2 From the **Format** menu, select **Cells**.

3 Click on the **Font** tab.

4 Click on the **Color** box.

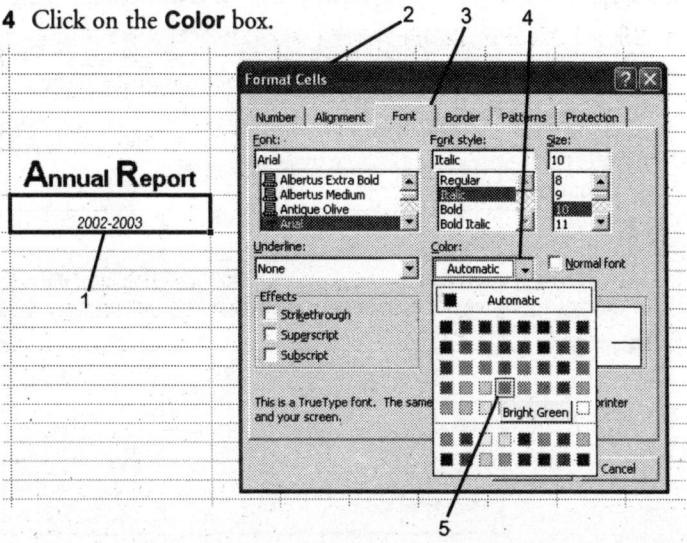

5 Click on a square in the colour chart.

6 Click on **OK**.

Or

1 Select a cell or mark a range.

2 Click on the arrow to the right of the button.

3 Click on a square in the colour chart.

To apply the same colour to another cell or range:

1 Select a cell or mark a range.

2 Click on the button. The line at the bottom of the button shows the colour that will be applied.

tip

> To change the colour depending on whether the content of the cell is a positive or negative number, zero or text, set up a custom format. See page 76.

Change the colour for text within a cell

Although you will usually want to apply colour to a whole cell, you can change the colour for just some of the characters in a cell that contains text. (You cannot change part of a cell if the cell has been given one of the number formats.)

1 Double-click on the cell to edit the contents.

2 Mark the characters you want to change by dragging the cursor over them.

3 Click on the arrow to the right of the ▲ button.

4 Click on a square in the colour chart.

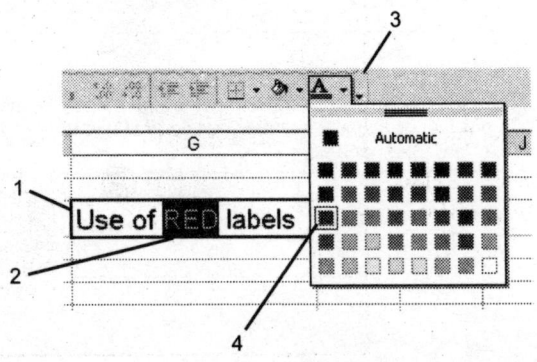

Change the colours used in the worksheet

Any of the colours on the colour chart can be replaced.

1 From the **Tools** menu, select **Options**.

2 Click on the **Color** tab.

3 Click on a square in the colour chart.

4 Click on the **Modify** button.

5 Click on a new colour and click on **OK**.

   Or

   Click on the **Custom** tab, choose a colour and click on **OK**.

6 Click on **OK** to close the Options dialog.

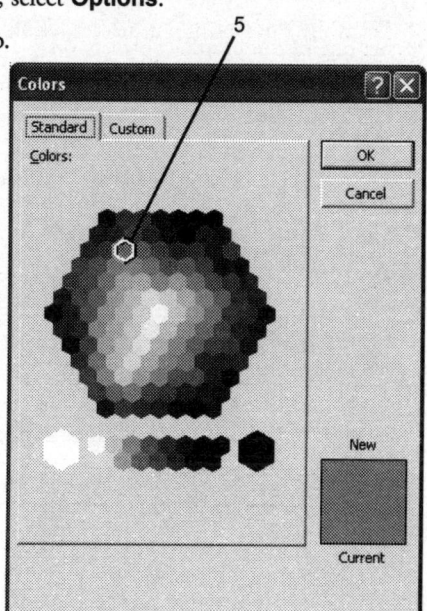

Add a border

You can mark out areas of the worksheet by drawing a border around them.

1 Select a cell or mark a range.

2 From the **Format** menu, select **Cells**.

3 Click on the **Border** tab.

4 Click on a line **Style** to select the line width or choose a dotted line.

5 Select a colour for the line.

6 Click on the border buttons to add lines to the cell borders.

   Or

   Click on the **Border** diagram where you want lines to appear.

   Or

   Click on one of the **Presets** buttons to draw a box around the edge of the whole area, add lines to all inside edges or remove all borders.

7 Click on **OK**.

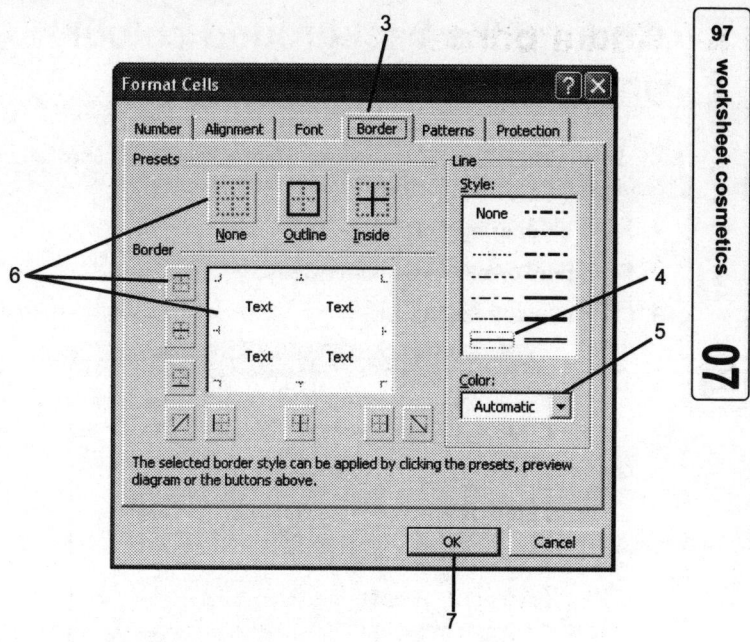

Or

1 Select a cell or mark a range.

2 Click on the arrow to the right of the ⊞ button.

3 Click on a border style in the drop-down chart.

Change the background colour and pattern

By default, the whole sheet is white. The background colour can be changed for any cell or range.

1 Select a cell or mark a range.

2 From the **Format** menu, select **Cells**.

3 Click on the **Patterns** tab.

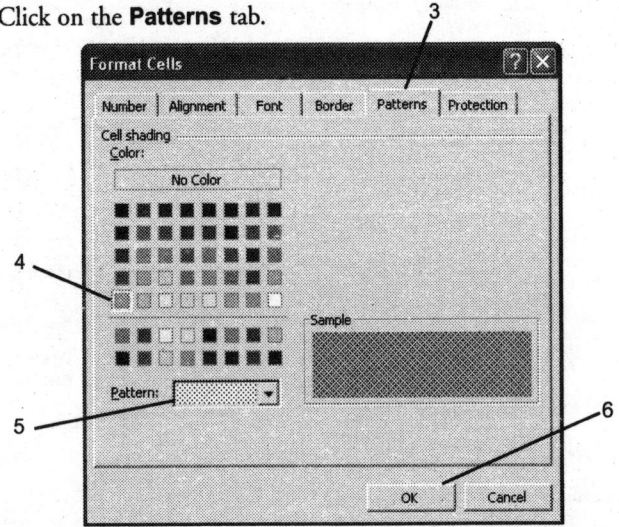

4 Choose a new background colour by clicking on a box in the colour chart. (To remove a background colour, click on **No Color**.)

5 If required, select a pattern from the **Pattern** drop-down box.

6 Click on **OK**.

Or

1 Select a cell or mark a range.

2 Click on the arrow to the right of the 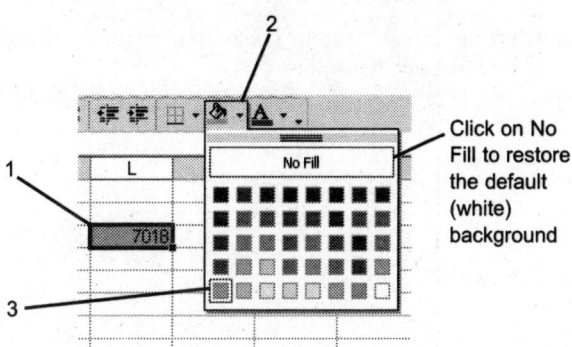 button.

3 Click on a background colour in the drop-down chart. (You cannot change the background pattern using this method.)

Click on No Fill to restore the default (white) background

Re-apply a border

To apply the most recently used border to another cell or range:

1 Select a cell or mark a range.

2 Click on the button. The button shows the border that will be applied.

Re-apply a background colour

To apply the most recently used background colour to another cell or range:

1 Select a cell or mark a range.

2 Click on the ⬦ button. The button shows the background colour that will be applied.

Hide the worksheet borders

When a worksheet is complete, its appearance can be improved by hiding the borders containing the row numbers and column letters.

1 From the **Tools** menu, select **Options**.

2 Click on the **View** tab.

3 Click on the **Row & column headers** check box to turn off the headers.

4 Click on **OK**.

To restore the borders, click on the check box again.

Click to turn labels on or off

Hide Excel worksheet features

The Excel display includes a title bar and toolbars at the top of the window and a status bar at the bottom. For display purposes, these can be hidden and the worksheet can be made to fill the whole screen.

To hide the Excel features, select **Full Screen** from the **View** menu. With the features hidden you can:

- Move around the sheet with the vertical scroll bar or the arrow keys.

- Enter, edit and delete data in cells.

	File Edit View Insert Format Tools Data Window Help					
	B	C	D	E	F	G
2						
3			**January 2003**			
4						
5		Date	Details	Credit	Debit	Balance
6						
7			O/Balance			152.90
8		01/01/03	Fuel		32.45	
9		01/03/03	Sundries		18.04	
10		01/04/03	Postage		5.20	
11		01/04/03	Fuel		17.90	
12		01/05/03	Postage		3.40	

- Use the Excel menus (still shown) or right-click to display a pop-up menu.

- Perform any other action that is carried out from within the worksheet itself.

To restore the title bar, toolbars and status bar, click on the **Close Full Screen** button.

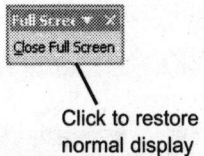

Click to restore
normal display

Zoom in on the worksheet

You can magnify the display or show more of the worksheet with the zoom options.

1 From the **View** menu, select **Zoom**.

2 Click on a **Magnification** option and then on **OK**.

Alternatively, select an option from the **Zoom** drop-down list on the toolbar.

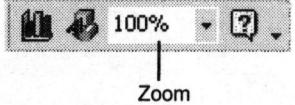

Zoom

Turn off the grid lines

The worksheet is normally displayed with horizontal and vertical grid lines dividing the cells. When borders and background colours have been applied, these grid lines can be turned off to give a clearer display.

1 From the **Tools** menu, select **Options**.

2 Click on the **View** tab.

3 Click on the **Gridlines** check box to turn off the lines.

4 Click on OK.

To restore the grid lines, click on the **Gridlines** check box again.

Click to turn grid lines on or off

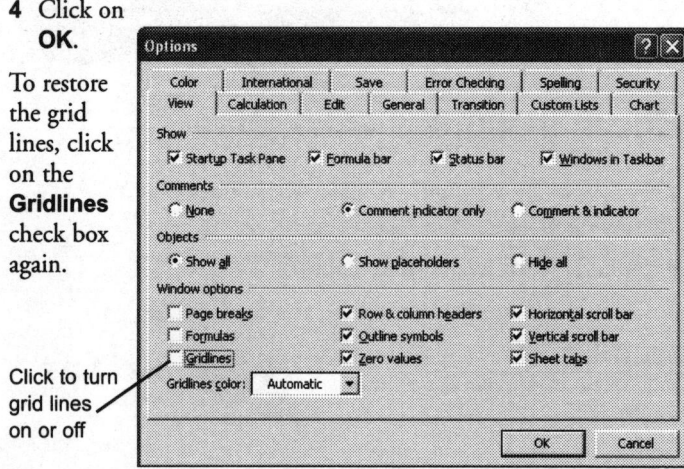

08
display formats and styles

Copy a display format

The number format, alignment, font, text colour, border and
background colour together make up the display format for a cell.
This format can be copied to other cells in the worksheet using the
Format Painter.

1 Click on a cell whose display format you want to duplicate.

2 Click on the  button on the toolbar.

Format Painter

3 Click on another cell or mark a range.

For a range with several different formats, use the Format Painter to
copy the formats to another range of the same size.

1 Mark the range whose display formats you want to duplicate.

2 Click on the ✎ button on the toolbar.

3 Mark a similar range. (If the range is a different size, the results
may not be as expected.)

Copy a display format several times

Display formats can be duplicated over any number of cells or ranges.

1 Click on a cell whose display format you want to duplicate.

2 Double-click on the ✍ button on the toolbar.

3 Click on each cell or mark each range where the display format is to be applied.

4 Click on the ✍ button again to end the process.

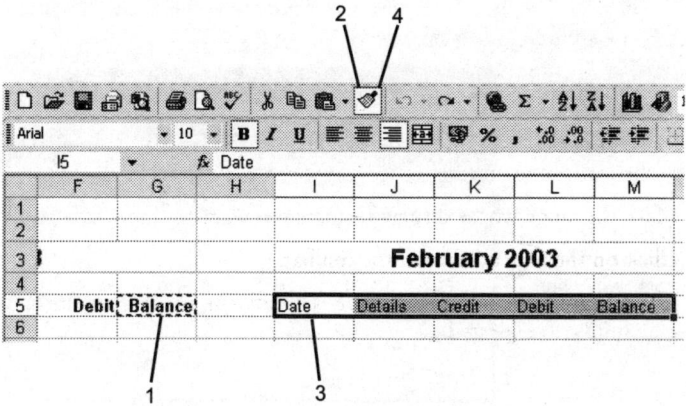

Create a format style

Rather than copy the display format from one cell to another with
the Format Painter, you can create a format style that can be
applied as often as you like. The style can include the whole display
format or just some of the features (such as the number format and
alignment).

1 Click on a cell containing the display format on which the style
   is to be based.

2 From the **Format** menu, select **Style**.

3 Type a name in the **Style name** box.

4 Click on the check boxes for any elements of the display format
   to be excluded from the style.

5 Click on
   OK.

The display
format elements
are shown when
you start typing
the new style
name

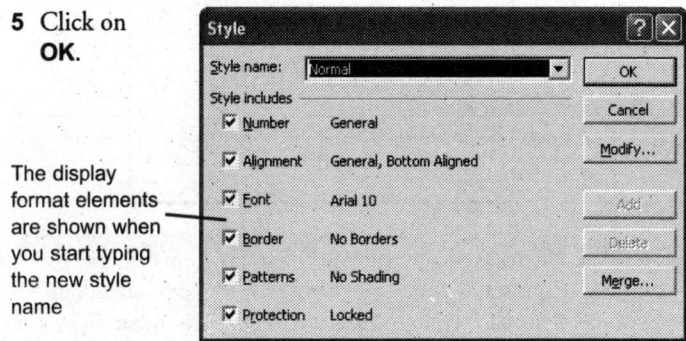

Apply a format style

To apply a stored format style to part of a worksheet:

1 Click on a cell or mark a range.

2 From the **Format** menu, select **Style**.

3 Select a style from the **Style name** drop-down list. The style details are shown in the main part of the dialog box.

4 Click on **OK**.

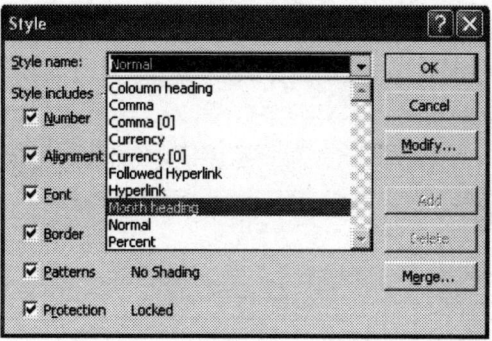

5 You can now override any part of the display format in any of the cells. For instance, you can change the background colour for individual cells, without affecting the style for other cells.

Modify a format style

A stored format style can be changed; all cells that have that style
are updated to reflect the changes.

1 From the **Format** menu, select **Style**.

2 Select a style from the **Style name** drop-down list.

3 Click on the **Modify** button.

4 The Format Cells dialog box is displayed. Make changes in each
   of the tabs, as required.

5 Click on **OK** to close the Format Cells dialog box.

6 Click on **OK** to close the Style dialog box.

tip

You cannot undo changes to a format style, so save the
worksheet before making the modifications.

Use the Normal style

Initially, the worksheet includes only the Normal style. This is applied to all cells on the worksheet until replaced with a customized style.

- You can modify the Normal style by selecting it in the Style dialog box and clicking on the **Modify** button. All cells that have not been assigned another format style are affected by the changes and modified accordingly.

- You can remove a customized style for a range (or cell) by marking the range and then selecting the Normal style.

- You cannot delete the Normal style.

Use the Style box

You can make the application of styles faster by adding the Style box to a toolbar.

1 From the **Tools** menu, select **Customize**.

2 On the **Commands** tab, select the **Format** category and drag the Style box onto a toolbar.

3 Click on **Close**.

Apply a style by selecting from this box; add a style by typing a new name in the Style box.

Delete a format style

Any of your format styles can be deleted:

1 From the **Format** menu, select **Style**.

2 Select a style from the **Style name** drop-down list.

3 Click on the **Delete** button. No confirmation is asked for, so make sure the correct style has been selected before clicking on the button.

4 Click on **OK**.

When you delete a style, the Normal style is applied to all cells that had the deleted style.

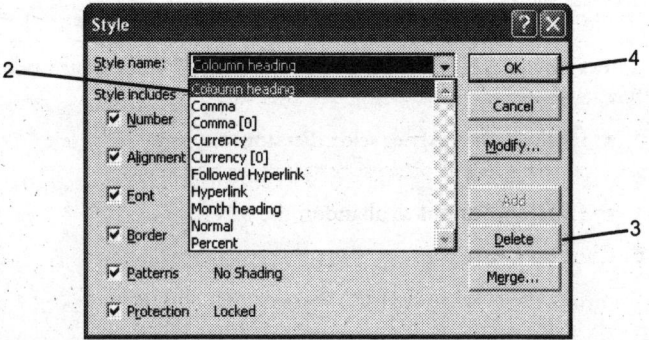

Merge format styles

Format styles from another worksheet can be added to the current worksheet.

1 Open the worksheet from which the styles are to be merged.

2 From the **Format** menu, select **Style**.

3 Click on the **Merge** button.

4 Click on the worksheet that has the required styles and click on **OK**.

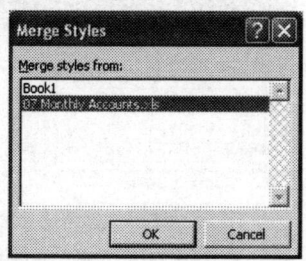

5 If any style names are the same in both sheets, you are asked for confirmation of the action to be taken:

- Click on **Yes** if the styles in the current worksheet are to be replaced by those on the selected sheet.

- Click on **No** if styles with the same name are to be left unchanged but other styles are to be added.

- Click on **Cancel** to abandon the merge.

6 Click on **OK**.

Apply an AutoFormat

Excel has some built-in formats that can be applied to a range of cells. These can be useful for certain standard worksheet designs.

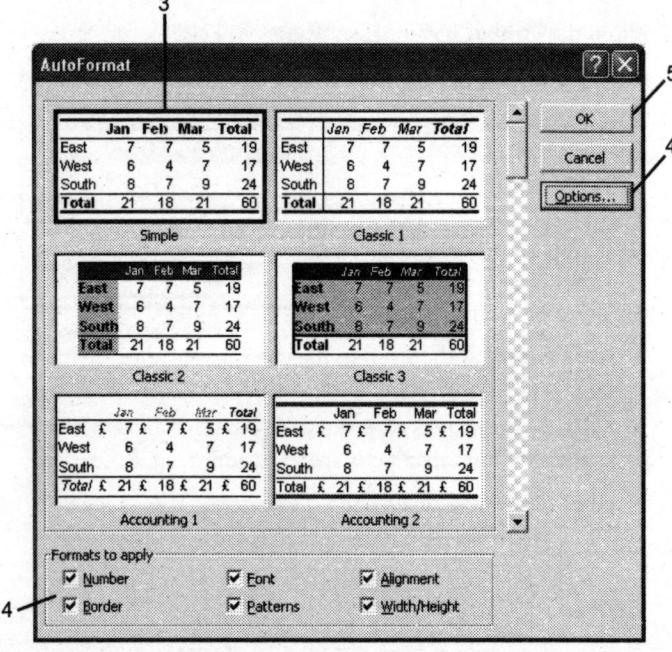

1 Mark the range to which the AutoFormat is to be applied.

2 From the **Format** menu, select **AutoFormat**.

3 Select an AutoFormat by clicking on it.

4 Click on the **Options** button if you want to apply only certain aspects of the format (e.g. the font or background colour). Turn off those elements you do not want by clicking on the check boxes.

5 Click on **OK**.

After you have applied an AutoFormat to a range of cells, you can change any of the formatting options for cells within the range. Therefore an AutoFormat is often a good starting point for designing your own format.

Apply conditional formatting

Using the Custom format, you can change the cell format and
colour depending on whether the value is positive, negative, zero or
text. You can also apply the complete range of formatting options
(including borders, patterns, fonts etc.) depending on a much more
sophisticated set of conditions.

1 Click on the cell or mark the range to which the conditional
format is to apply.

2 From the **Format** menu, select **Conditional Formatting**.

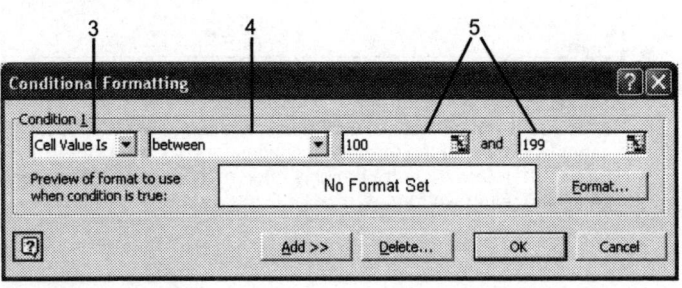

3 Choose whether the formatting is to depend on the value of a
cell or a formula.

4 Choose the type of condition to be applied (e.g. the cell value is
between two specified numbers or greater than a given value).

5 Give the value or values against which the cell is to be compared. (You may enter a formula here: see page 119.)

6 Click on the **Format** button and set the format to be applied if the condition is true.

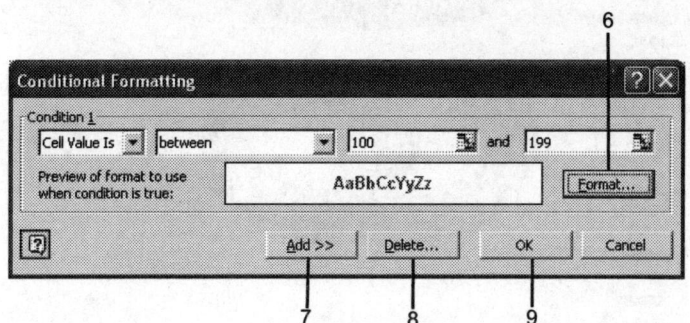

7 Click on **Add** if you want to apply a further condition and formatting for the cell (for instance, to use one colour for positive amounts and another for negative values).

8 Click on **Delete** to delete one of the conditions.

9 Click on **OK**.

As the values change in the selected cells, the format is updated accordingly.

09

formulae and functions

Use a formula

Excel formulae allow you to calculate the value of a cell from the contents of other cells. For example, a cell can hold the difference between two other cells or the sum of a range.

A formula consists of a +, - or = symbol followed by an expression. The expression is one or more cell references or values separated by operators (such as + and -). For example:

= B4 + B5

The value of the cell containing this formula would be the total of the values in cells B4 and B5.

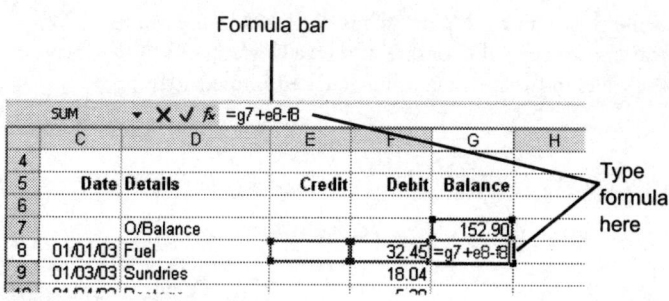

Formula bar

Type formula here

Enter a formula

To enter a formula:

1 Click on the cell where the formula is to be entered.

2 Type the formula.

3 Press **[Enter]** or move to another cell.

tip

Spaces in formulae are ignored so can be used to make the formula more readable.

Cell references can be typed in either capitals or lower case letters. As you type the formula, any referenced cells are highlighted in different colours.

When you click on a cell, the formula is shown in the formula bar, while the result of the formula is displayed in the cell itself. When you change the value of one of the cells referenced in the formula, the value in the formula cell is updated immediately.

Formula shown in formula bar

	G8	▾	*fx* =G7+E8-F8				
	C	D	E	F	G	H	
4							
5	Date	Details	Credit	Debit	Balance		
6							
7		O/Balance			152.90		Result
8	01/01/03	Fuel		32.45	120.45		shown
9	01/03/03	Sundries		18.04			in cell
10	01/04/02	Postage		5.20			

Edit a formula

To edit a formula:

1 Click on the cell containing the formula.

2 Click inside the formula bar. Any cell references in the formula are shown in different colours and the corresponding cells are temporarily given the same colours.

3 Make the changes by typing and using the **[Delete]** and **[Backspace]** keys.

4 Press **[Enter]**.

The result of the formula is shown immediately.

tip

If the result of a formula is shown as #VALUE! there is some error in the formula, so it cannot be calculated. When you click on the cell a warning symbol is displayed; clicking on this symbol gives you a menu of options. You can edit the formula in the usual way.

Use the mouse to specify references

You can use the mouse to identify cells or ranges when entering or editing a formula.

To add a formula using the mouse:

1 Click on the cell where the formula is to be entered.

2 Type the formula to the point where a reference is required.

3 Click on the cell or mark the range that is to be included in the formula.

4 Type the rest of the formula (marking other cells or ranges as necessary).

5 Press **[Enter]**.

To edit a formula using the mouse:

1 Click on the cell containing the formula to be edited.

2 Click inside the formula bar.

3 Delete the incorrect cell or range reference using the **[Delete]** and **[Backspace]** keys.

3 Click on the replacement cell or mark the new range.

4 Press **[Enter]**.

Delete a formula

A cell containing a formula can be changed in the same way as any other cell:

- To remove a formula, click on the cell and press **[Delete]**.
- To replace a formula with a value or a different formula, click on the cell and type the new value or formula.

Always check that the results of a formula are reasonable. If you are intending to copy a formula to other locations on the worksheet, check the result manually so that you are sure the formula is accurate and the correct references have been used; otherwise, you will end up repeating the same error all over your worksheet. If in doubt, delete the formula and start again.

Use operators in formulae

Excel formulae can contain any of the following operators:

+	Add numbers
-	Subtract
*	Multiply
/	Divide
^	Raise to a power (e.g. $5\wedge2 = 5^2 = 25$)
&	Combine text values

You can also put a - sign in front of a number to negate it. For example:

= B4 * -2

This formula multiplies the contents of B4 by -2.

Similarly, you can use a % symbol after a number to calculate a percentage. For example:

= C5 * 10%

This gives a result that is 10% of the value in cell C5.

Within a formula, the operators are handled in a particular order. The order of calculation is as follows:

- %   Negation and percentage

^   Raising to a power

* /   Multiplication and division

+ -   Addition and subtraction

For example:

= 5 + B7 * 25%

This formula takes 25% of the value in B7 and then adds 5 (rather than adding 5 to B7 and then taking 25% of the total).

The order of calculation can be changed using brackets (see page 126).

Note the following when using text in formulae:

- You cannot mix numeric and text operators in a formula.

- If you want to combine two items of text, you must use the & operator; you cannot use + to add one item of text to another.

Insert brackets to change the calculation order

You can change the way in which a formula is calculated by inserting brackets in the formula. Excel calculates everything inside the brackets first.

You can have more than one set of brackets in a formula, and one pair can contain another. Calculation starts with the inside brackets. For example:

$$= ((C4 + 1) * (C5 + 1)) / C7$$

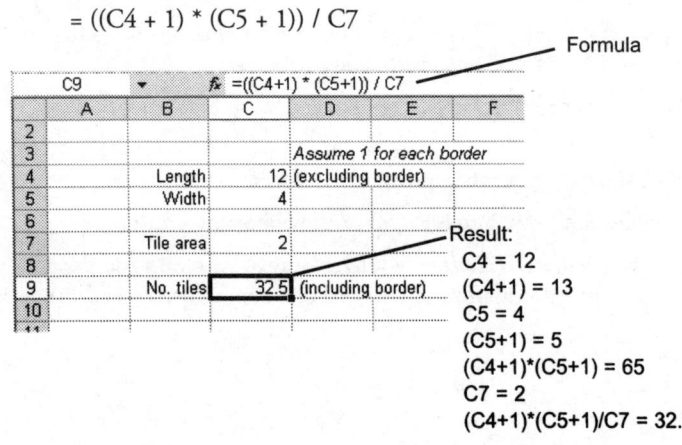

Formula

Result:
C4 = 12
(C4+1) = 13
C5 = 4
(C5+1) = 5
(C4+1)*(C5+1) = 65
C7 = 2
(C4+1)*(C5+1)/C7 = 32.5

Here, the formula adds 1 to the value of C4, adds 1 to C5, then multiplies the two results together before finally dividing by C7. (Strictly speaking, the outer pair of brackets are not necessary in this example but they help to make the formula clearer.)

If you now change the values in cells C4 and C5, you will get a different result in C7.

The process of putting one pair of brackets inside another is called 'nesting'. You can nest up to seven levels of brackets in one formula, though finding errors in the formula then becomes extremely difficult. It is better to split up complex formulae, putting intermediate values in other cells.

When you edit a formula and move the cursor onto a bracket, the corresponding bracket in the formula is highlighted. Brackets must always be in matching pairs.

Copy a formula

A formula can be copied in the same way as a simple value. However, the formula is modified so that it refers to cells in the same relative position. For example, if a formula adds the numbers in the column above it, when you copy the formula the new version will add the numbers above the new cell.

References to cells in a formula are called 'relative' references because, when copied, they refer to cells in the same relative position.

	G9	▾	ƒ	=G8+E9-F9	
	C	D	E	F	G
4					
5	Date	Details	Credit	Debit	Balance
6					
7		O/Balance			152.90
8	01/01/03	Fuel		32.45	120.45
9	01/03/03	Sundries		18.04	102.41
10	01/04/03	Postage		5.20	97.21
11	01/04/03	Fuel		17.90	79.31
12	01/05/03	Postage		2.40	76.91
13	01/07/03	Travel		22.75	54.16
14	01/09/03	Fuel		30.08	24.08
15	01/09/03	Postage		10.90	13.18
16	01/09/03	Transfer	300.00		313.18
17	01/10/03	Books		54.98	258.20
18					

Original formula: =G7+E8-F8

Copied formula: =G8+E9-F9

Copied formula: =G16+E17-F17

To copy a formula:

1 Click on the cell containing the formula or mark the range.

2 Press **[Ctrl] + [C]** to copy the formula to the clipboard.

3 Click on the cell or mark the range where you want the copy to appear.

4 Press **[Enter]** to copy the formula to the new position.

Move a formula

To move a formula:

1 Click on the cell containing the formula or mark the range.

2 Press **[Ctrl] + [X]** to copy the formula to the clipboard.

3 Click on the cell or mark the range where you want to move the formula.

4 Press **[Enter]** to move the formula to the new position.

The relative references are not updated. To move a formula but update the references, copy the formula and then delete the original.

Use absolute cell references

Sometimes you will want to copy a formula but still refer to the original cells. For example, an invoice may apply a fixed discount to a whole column of values. To do this you must use 'absolute' cell references.

An absolute cell reference has $ signs in front of each part of the reference. For example, a formula my be entered in cell E5 as follows:

= D5 * B1

If this formula is copied to cell F6 it will become:

= E6 * B1

Wherever you copy the formula, it will always refer to cell B1.

You can also fix the reference for just the row or column by including only one $ sign. For example, $F1 fixes the column as F but allows the row (initially row 1) to change. Similarly, F$1 fixes the row but changes the column.

In the example below, the main block of data is based on a single formula, entered in E9:

= $D9 * E$7

When this formula is copied across the row it becomes:

= $D9 * F$7 in cell F9
= $D9 * G$7 in cell G9

Similarly, when copied down column E the only part that changes is '$D9'. In this way, the formula in each cell takes the value from the corresponding cell in column D and multiplies it by the exchange rate at the top of the column (in row 7).

	C	D	E	F	G	H
4						
5			£	$	€	
6		Exchange				
7		Rate	1.0000	1.5546	1.5924	
8						
9		1.00	1.00	1.55	1.59	
10		2.00	2.00	3.11	3.18	
11		3.00	3.00	4.66	4.78	
12	Current	4.00	4.00	6.22	6.37	
13	Value	5.00	5.00	7.77	7.96	
14		6.00	6.00	9.33	9.55	
15		7.00	7.00	10.88	11.15	
16		8.00	8.00	12.44	12.74	
17		9.00	9.00	13.99	14.33	
18		10.00	10.00	15.55	15.92	
19						

=$D9*G$7

=$D18*E$7

=$D18*G$7

Use a function in a formula

Functions are used in formulae to complete specific tasks that cannot be performed by simple formulae. For example, the SUM function gives you the total of the cells in a range; LEN returns the length of an item of text.

A function consists of the function name, followed by a pair of brackets containing the function's *argument*. The argument is the value that the function uses to calculate the result: for example, the range to be totalled or the cell containing the text for which the length is to be calculated.

	A	B	C	D
1				
2				
3				
4				
5			23.4	
6			19.5	
7			27.2	
8			46.9	
9			123.5	
10				
11		TOTAL	240.5	
12				

Formula:
=SUM(C5:C9)

Function   Argument

Some functions require two or more arguments. In these cases the arguments are separated by commas.

Where the argument is a range, this consists of the top left-hand and bottom right-hand cells, separated by a colon (e.g. A1:D6).

You can use any expression as the argument; for instance, the result of one function can be the argument for another.

	A	B	C	D	E
14					
15		**Name**	**Length**	**Code**	
16		Bristol	7	BRI	
17		Leeds	5	LEE	
18		Manchester	10	MAN	
19		Norfolk	7	NOR	
20		Salisbury	9	SAL	
21					

Formula in D20:
=UPPER(LEFT(B20, 3))

Formula in C20:
=LEN(B20)

Argument of UPPER function:
LEFT(B20, 3)

Functions used:
LEN (Length of text)
UPPER (Converts to upper case)
LEFT (Extracts left-hand portion)

Arguments of LEFT function:
B20 (cell containing text)
3 (amount of text required)

Add a function

When adding a function to a formula, you can either type the function completely or mark any cells or ranges with the mouse.

To add a function using the mouse:

1 Type the function name and opening bracket. A pop-up label reminds you of the arguments you need.

2 Click on the cell or mark the range that forms the first argument.

3 If there is more than one argument, type a comma.

4 Add further arguments and commas as necessary.

5 Type the closing bracket.

	SUM	▾ ✗ ✓ *fx*	=sum(C5:C9			
	A	B	C	D	E	F
3						
4						
5			23.4			
6			19.5			
7			27.2			
8			46.9			
9			123.5			
10						
11		TOTAL	=sum(C5:C9			
12			SUM(**number1**, [number2], ...)			

Use the SUM function

The SUM function returns the total of one or more ranges. If there is more than one range, these must be separated by commas.

For a single range, you can either type the function directly or use the AutoSum button.

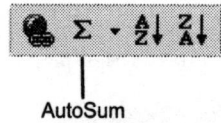

AutoSum

1 Click on the cell that is to contain the total.

2 Click on the Σ button on the toolbar.

3 Excel makes a guess at the range to be totalled. If this is wrong, mark the correct range.

4 Press **[Enter]**.

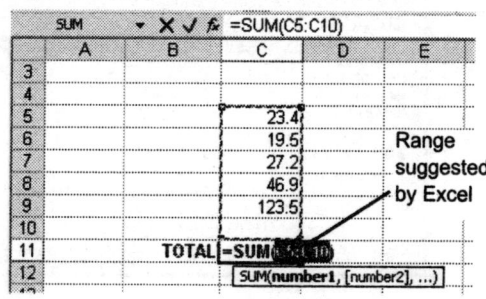

Use the Insert Function dialog box

Although you can type in any function directly, provided you know what arguments it requires, Excel includes the Insert Function dialog box to make the task easier.

1 Start typing the formula until you reach the place where the function is required.

2 Click on the 𝑓𝑥 button to the left of the formula bar. The Insert Function dialog box is displayed.

Insert Function

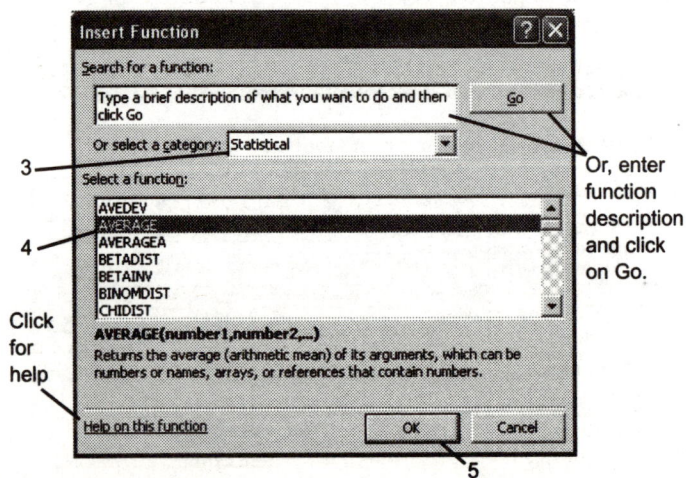

Or, enter function description and click on Go.

Click for help

3 — Or select a category: Statistical

4 — AVERAGE

5 — OK

3 A box in the top portion of the dialog box lets you select from a list of categories of built-in functions supplied with Excel. Select a category. If you are not sure which category the function is in, select 'All'.

4 The bottom half of the dialog box lists the functions for the selected category. Click on the function name. A description is shown at the bottom of the dialog box.

5 Click on **OK**. Another dialog box allows you to enter the function arguments.

6 Enter the arguments, either by typing them directly or by marking cells or ranges.

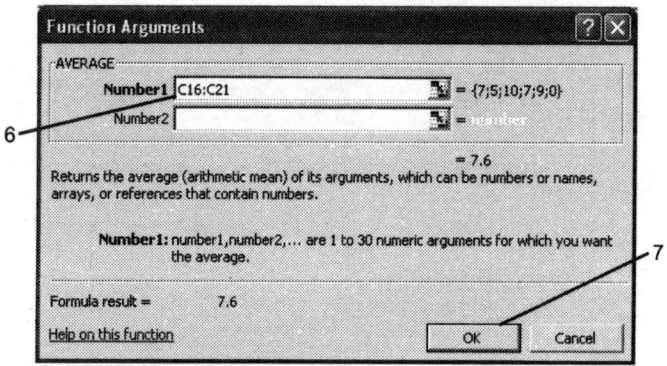

7 Click on **OK** to add the function to the formula.

Use numeric functions

Excel includes a large number of numeric and financial functions:

- The **Financial** category includes functions such as RATE (interest rate per period of a loan) and NPV (net present value).

- The **Math & Trig** category includes various mathematical functions, such as SUM, ABS (absolute value, ignoring any minus sign) and INT (integer part of number); and trigonometry functions, such as SIN (sine), COS (cosine) and ATN (arctangent).

- The **Statistical** category includes functions ranging from the simple AVERAGE and MAX functions to more sophisticated options such as STDEV (standard deviation) and BINOMDIST (binomial distribution).

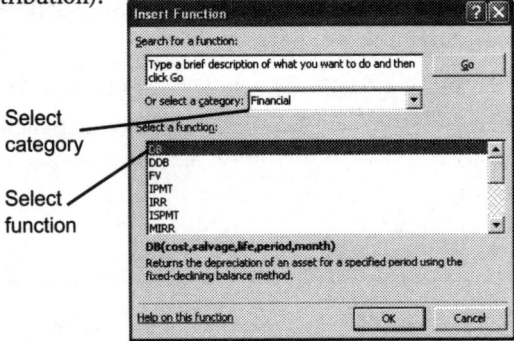

Select category

Select function

Use date and time functions

The **Date & Time** category on the Insert Function dialog box provides all the functions you need for working with dates and times:

- NOW has no arguments and returns the current date and time, as held by the computer. TODAY returns the current date.

- DATE returns a date value for a given year, month and day; TIME returns a time value for a given hour, minute and second.

- DATEVALUE and TIMEVALUE convert text dates and times into their equivalent numeric values.

- DAY returns the day of the month for a date/time value; other elements of the value can be found with MONTH and YEAR. Similarly, HOUR, MINUTE and SECOND can be used to extract the time elements.

- WEEKDAY returns a number representing the day of the week.

For details of how dates and times are stored on the worksheet, see page 84.

Use text functions

The **Text** category contains a large number of functions for manipulating text. For example:

- LEN returns the length of a piece of text.

- LEFT, RIGHT and MID return a section of text from the left, right or middle of the specified text.

- TRIM removes spaces from either end of a piece of text.

- UPPER and LOWER convert text to capitals or lower case.

- FIND searches one piece of text for another.

- CODE returns the ASCII code for a character; CHAR converts a number into its equivalent ASCII character.

Select category

Select function

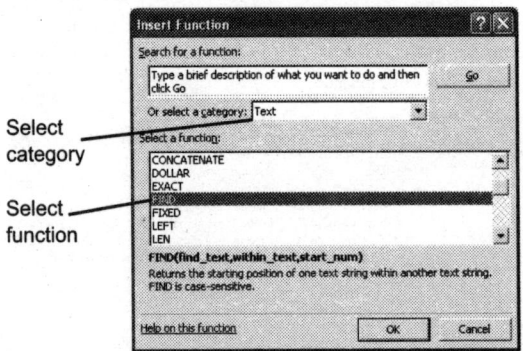

Use other functions

As well as the categories described above, Excel includes a variety of functions in several categories for more unusual formulae:

- The **Lookup & Reference** functions let you search a table of data for a given value and perform other, related operations.

- The **Database** functions perform actions on database records.

- The **Logical** functions perform logical operations, returning values of TRUE or FALSE; most usefully, the category includes the IF function (see page 142).

- The **Information** functions return information about the cells themselves (such as whether they contain a number or an error).

	A	B	C	D	E	F
1						
2			Examples of the CELL function			
3						
4			Argument 1	Result	Formula	Effect
5						
6	Sample		address	A6	=CELL("address",A6)	Address of cell
7	Sample		col	1	=CELL("col",A7)	Column number
8	Sample		contents	Sample	=CELL("contents",A8)	Contents of cell
9	Sample		format	G	=CELL("format",A9)	Format code (G = General etc.)
10	Sample		prefix	'	=CELL("prefix",A10)	Type of text format (' left, " right, ^ centre etc.)
11	Sample		type	l	=CELL("type",A11)	Type of data (b blank, l text, v value)
12	Sample		width	8	=CELL("width",A12)	Column width (to nearest whole number)
13						

Apply the IF function

The IF function allows you to set the value of a cell depending on the outcome of a condition. For example, you might calculate a tax percentage from a tax code.

The function has three arguments:

- The condition
- The return value for a TRUE condition
- The return value for a FALSE condition

The condition compares one expression against another; for example, the expression 'B7 = 0' returns a TRUE value if B7 contains zero or is blank, FALSE otherwise. You can use the following comparison operators:

=	Equal
<>	Not equal
<	Less than
<=	Less or equal
>	Greater than
>=	Greater or equal

You can also combine conditions with the following operators:

AND   Condition is TRUE if both parts are TRUE.

OR   Condition is TRUE if one or both parts are TRUE.

D	E	F	G	H	I	J
	Net	VAT Rate	VAT %	VAT Amount	Gross	
	120.56	0	0	0	120.56	
	203.78	1	17.5	35.66	239.44	
	43.00	1	17.5	7.52	50.52	
	1004.00	0	0	0	1004.00	
	89.99	1	17.5	15.74	105.73	

Formula:
=IF(F8=0,0,17.5)

If F8=0,
function returns 0;
otherwise returns 17.5

Formula:
=(INT(E8*G8))/100

Formula:
=E8+H8

You can also *nest* one IF function inside another. For example:

IF(F8=0, 0, (IF F8=1, 17.5, "*ERROR*"))

If F8 contains 0, the result is 0; otherwise, if F8 contains 1, the result is 17.5; in all other cases the result is the text '*ERROR*'.

Get help with functions

The Insert Function dialog box gives a brief description of the selected function but in some cases you will need more than that. For example, the CELL function has a long list of possible arguments and some of these return codes that are not intuitive. In such cases you can get further help.

1 In the Insert Function dialog box, click on **Help on this function**.

2 In the Office Assistant options, click on **Help with this option**.

3 Click on **Help on selected function**. The relevant help topic is displayed.

4 After viewing the help, click on the ▣ button.

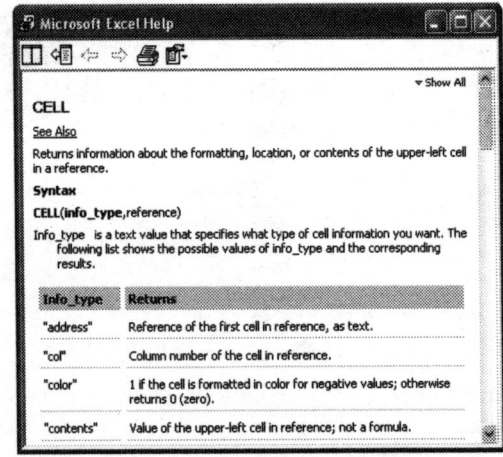

Microsoft Excel Help

▾ Show All

CELL

See Also

Returns information about the formatting, location, or contents of the upper-left cell in a reference.

Syntax

CELL(info_type,reference)

Info_type is a text value that specifies what type of cell information you want. The following list shows the possible values of info_type and the corresponding results.

info_type	Returns
"address"	Reference of the first cell in reference, as text.
"col"	Column number of the cell in reference.
"color"	1 if the cell is formatted in color for negative values; otherwise returns 0 (zero).
"contents"	Value of the upper-left cell in reference; not a formula.

10

calculation options

Change the calculation method

When you change the value of any cell, Excel immediately recalculates all formulae that use that cell. If the results are used elsewhere, those formulae are recalculated, and so on.

You can change the way in which these calculations are done. Excel offers three alternatives:

- **Automatic** recalculation is the default and performs all calculations immediately.

- **Automatic except tables** recalculates everything in the worksheet except data tables.

- **Manual** recalculation turns off the automatic calculation. Each time you want to recalculate the sheet you must press **[F9]**.

To change the calculation method:

1 From the **Tools** menu, select **Options**.

2 Click on the **Calculation** tab.

3 Click on the required **Calculation** option.

4 If you have chosen **Manual** calculation, check that the **Recalculate before save** box is turned on so that the sheet is recalculated each time it is saved; otherwise, the sheet will be saved with incorrect results.

5 Click on **OK**.

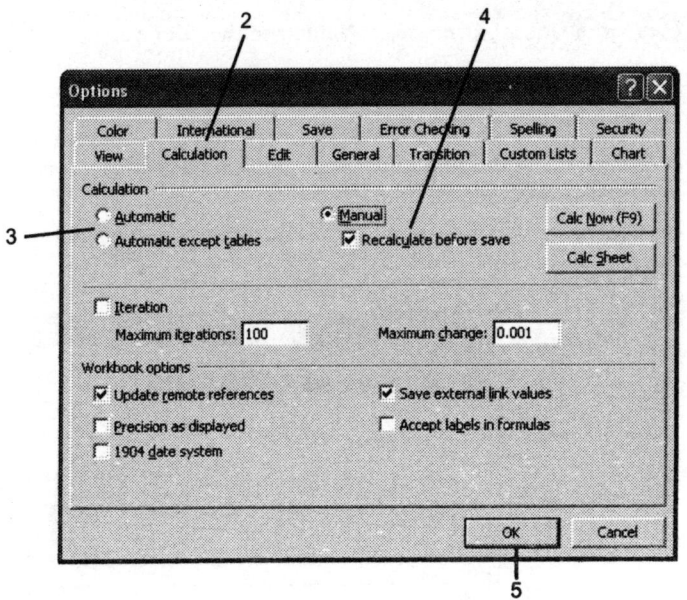

Name a cell or range

To make a formula more understandable, you can attach names to specific cells or ranges.

1 Click on the cell or mark the range to be named.

2 From the **Insert** menu, select **Name** and then **Define**.

3 If there is a text cell adjacent to the area to be named, Excel suggests this as the name. Enter a different name if this is not acceptable. Names must consist of letters, numbers, underscore characters and full stops; they must not contain any spaces and must start with a letter or underscore.

4 Click on **OK**.

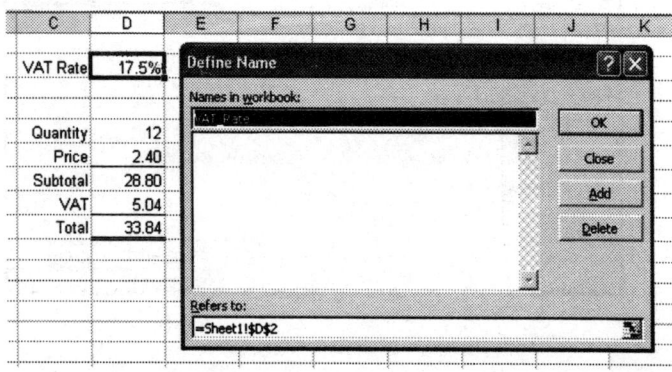

Name a group of cells

You can use a series of labels from the sheet as the names for a corresponding group of cells.

1 Mark a range including the cells to be named and their labels.

2 From the **Insert** menu, select **Name** and then **Create**.

3 Identify the position of the labels relative to the cells (e.g. choose **Left column** if the labels are in the column to the left of the values).

4 Click on **OK**.

Create Names

Create names in
- [ ] Top row
- [x] Left column
- [ ] Bottom row
- [ ] Right column

OK   Cancel

Click to list names on worksheet

Name shown, rather than cell reference

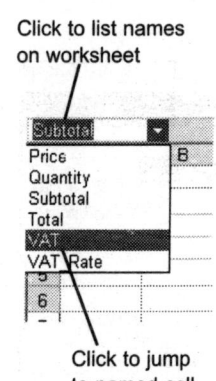

	Subtotal				
	Price		B		
	Quantity				
	Subtotal				
	Total				
	VAT				
	VAT Rate				
5					
6					

Click to jump to named cell

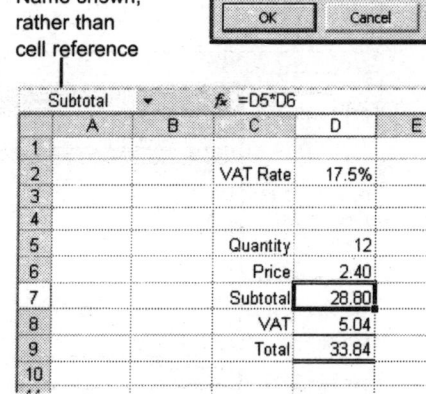

Subtotal	▾	fx =D5*D6		
	A	B	C	D	E
1					
2			VAT Rate	17.5%	
3					
4					
5			Quantity	12	
6			Price	2.40	
7			Subtotal	28.80	
8			VAT	5.04	
9			Total	33.84	
10					

Use a name in a formula

When you have named a cell or range, you can use the name in a formula by replacing the cell or range reference with the name.

To insert a name using the mouse:

1 Type the formula to the point where a reference is required.

2 Click on the named cell or mark the range that is to be included in the formula. The name is inserted in the formula.

	AVERAGE	▾ ✗ ✓ ƒ×	=Quantity*Price		
	A	B	C	D	E
1					
2			VAT Rate	17.5%	
3					
4					
5			Quantity	12	
6			Price	2.40	
7			Subtotal	=Quantity*Price	
8			VAT	5.04	
9			Total	33.84	
10					

Click on cell while typing formula

Cell name shown in formula

3 Type the rest of the formula (marking other cells or ranges as necessary).

4 Press **[Enter]**.

When you click on a cell, the formula in the formula bar now shows the cell or range names.

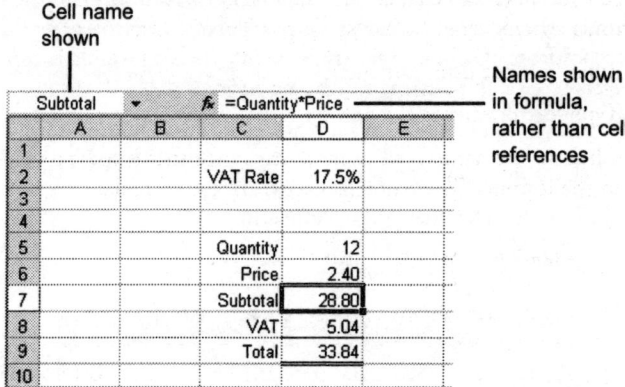

Cell name shown

Names shown in formula, rather than cell references

	A	B	C	D	E
1					
2			VAT Rate	17.5%	
3					
4					
5			Quantity	12	
6			Price	2.40	
7			Subtotal	28.80	
8			VAT	5.04	
9			Total	33.84	
10					

Subtotal f_x =Quantity*Price

tip

Each name has a cell or range reference attached to it. By default, this is an absolute reference, so if you copy a formula containing names to another location it will still refer to the original cells. This makes named cells and ranges particularly useful for circumstances where the same data values occur in a number of formulae throughout the sheet.

Change the reference for a name

You can change the cells attached to a name, which will affect any formulae that include the name. In particular, you can change the reference from absolute to relative, so that when a formula is copied it refers to cells in the same relative position.

1 From the **Insert** menu, select **Name** and then **Define**.

2 Click on the name you want to change.

3 Change the reference in the **Refers to** box.

4 Click on **OK**.

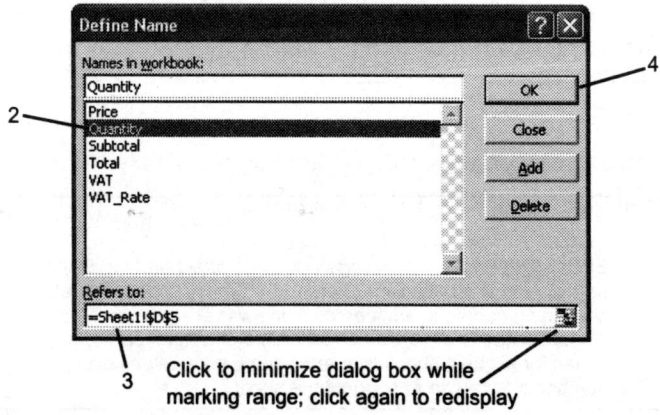

Click to minimize dialog box while
marking range; click again to redisplay

Delete a name

If you delete a name, you must edit any formulae that referred to the name.

1 From the **Insert** menu, select **Name** and then **Define**.

2 Click on the name you want to delete.

3 Click on the **Delete** box.

4 Click on **OK**.

Apply names to formulae

After adding names, you can apply these to any existing formulae. Cell and range references are replaced by names.

1 Mark the range containing the formulae.

2 From the **Insert** menu, select **Name** and then **Apply**.

3 Click on one or more names to be applied.

4 Click on **OK**. The formulae are updated.

Protect data from change

You can protect a worksheet against accidental damage by specifying that only selected areas of the sheet can be modified by a user. (All cells containing formulae will still be updated.)

The first stage is to identify those parts of the sheet where changes will be allowed. By default, when a sheet is protected, all cells are locked (so no change can be made).

1 Click on the cell or mark the range where changes are to be allowed.

2 From the **Format** menu, select **Cells**.

3 Click on the **Protection** tab.

4 Clear the **Locked** box.

5 Click on **OK**.

6 Repeat for other cells or ranges.

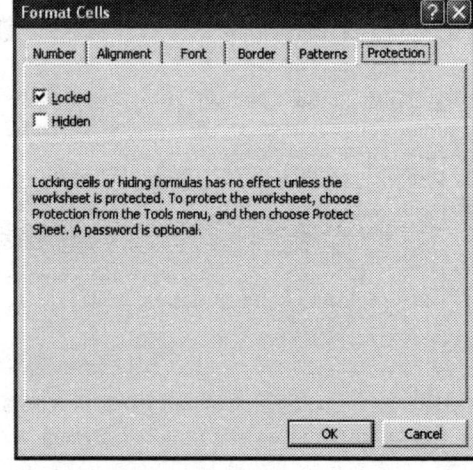

Format Cells

Number | Alignment | Font | Border | Patterns | Protection

☑ Locked
☐ Hidden

Locking cells or hiding formulas has no effect unless the worksheet is protected. To protect the worksheet, choose Protection from the Tools menu, and then choose Protect Sheet. A password is optional.

OK | Cancel

The second stage is to turn on protection for the whole sheet.

1 From the **Tools** menu, select **Protection** and then **Protect Sheet**.

2 If required, enter a password. (If you do this, users will have to enter the password before they are allowed to make any changes at all.)

3 Set the options according to what users will be allowed to do.

4 Click on **OK**.

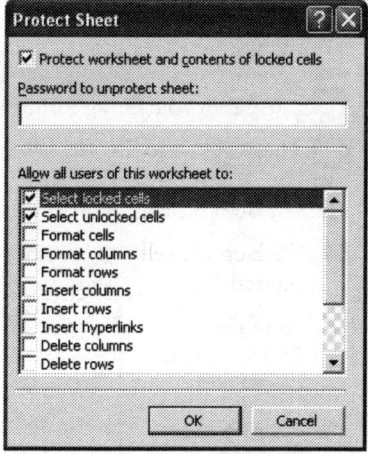

Any attempts to change locked areas of the worksheet now result in a warning message.

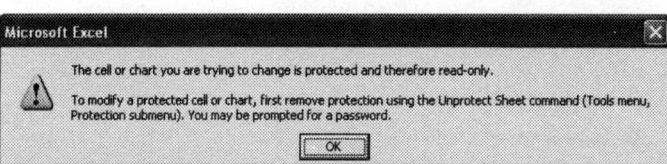

To turn protection off again: from the **Tools** menu, select **Protection** and then **Unprotect Sheet**.

11

workbooks and windows

Select a worksheet

The sheet you have created is part of a *workbook*, which is a collection of worksheets. The workbook is saved in the Excel file and provides a way of keeping related worksheets together.

The worksheets in the workbook are identified by the tabs at the bottom of the worksheet window. Initially, there are three tabs, labelled Sheet1, Sheet2 and Sheet3.

- To work with a different worksheet, click on the appropriate tab (e.g. Sheet2). You can now enter data and formulae, independently of the other sheets.

- To return to your first worksheet, click on the Sheet1 tab again.

When you save the file, all the worksheets are saved together. The latest changes to all worksheets are saved, even for those sheets you cannot currently see.

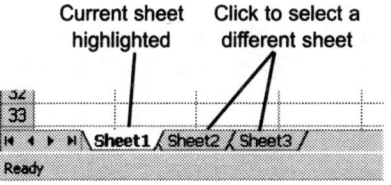

Current sheet highlighted   Click to select a different sheet

Rename a worksheet

If you have more than one worksheet in a workbook, you should give each of your worksheets a meaningful name.

1 Double-click on the sheet tab at the bottom of the worksheet window.

2 Type a name for the sheet. The name can contain any characters, including spaces, and may be up to 31 characters long.

3 Press **[Enter]**.

Double-click and
type new name

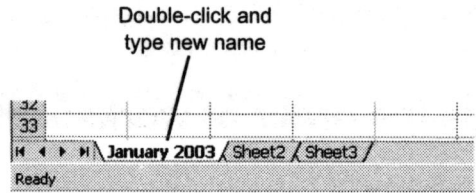

The name that you type relates to the worksheet only. The filename (shown in the title bar) stays the same and is the name for the whole workbook.

Add a worksheet to the workbook

If you need more than three worksheets in a workbook, you can add new ones at any time.

1 Click on the tab for an existing worksheet.

2 From the **Insert** menu, select **Worksheet**.

3 Double-click on the new sheet tab and give the worksheet a name.

New worksheet is inserted to left of selected tab

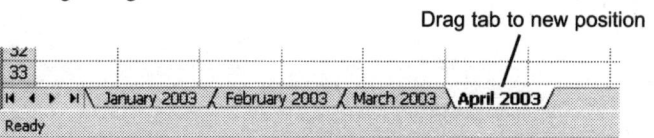

Change the order of worksheets

To change the order of the worksheet tabs:

1 Click on a sheet tab.

2 Drag the tab to its new position (between two other tabs or at the beginning or end of the tab bar).

Drag tab to new position

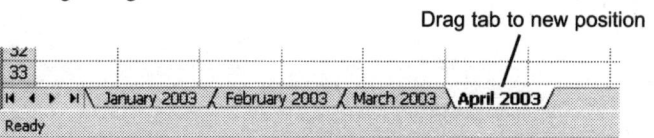

Select several worksheets

Some operations require you to select several worksheets at once.

1 Click on a sheet tab.

2 Hold down **[Shift]** and click on another tab. All intermediate tabs are selected.

Or

Hold down **[Ctrl]** and click on individual tabs to select a group of sheets that are not necessarily consecutive.

Selected tabs highlighted

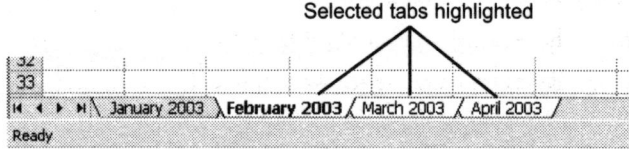

tip

Always save your work before carrying out any major tasks, such as deleting a sheet; the Undo option does not always work after such operations.

Select all worksheets

To select all the worksheets in the workbook:

1 Click on any sheet tab.
2 Right-click and choose **Select All Sheets** from the pop-up menu.

To select just one worksheet again, click on a different sheet tab.

Add several worksheets

To add several worksheets at once:

1 Mark the required number of existing tabs.
2 From the **Insert** menu, select **Worksheet**. The worksheets are added to the left of the first marked tab.
3 Rename each sheet.
4 Select the group of new sheet tabs and drag them to their new position.

Show different sheet tabs

As the number of worksheets in a workbook increases, you will not
be able to see all the sheet tabs at once. The four buttons to the left
of the tabs let you scroll through the tabs. (Note that clicking on
one of these buttons does not select a different worksheet.)

You can also change the way in which the bar at the bottom of the
worksheet window is divided between the sheet tabs and the
worksheet scroll bar. Drag the divider between the two sections of
the bar to the left or right to change the proportions.

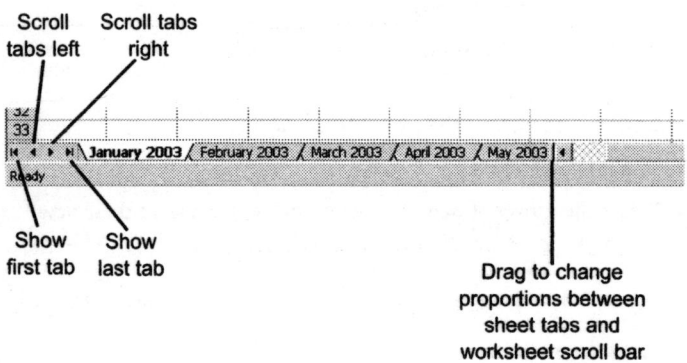

Scroll   Scroll tabs
tabs left   right

Show   Show
first tab   last tab

Drag to change
proportions between
sheet tabs and
worksheet scroll bar

Copy a worksheet

The worksheets within a workbook will often be similar in design. Therefore you can use one worksheet as the basis for another; a new worksheet can be created by copying an existing worksheet and then amending the copy. To copy a worksheet:

1 Click on the sheet tab of the worksheet to be copied.

2 Hold down **[Ctrl]** and drag the sheet tab to its new position.

An exact copy of the worksheet is created. You can change data and formulae in the new worksheet without affecting the original.

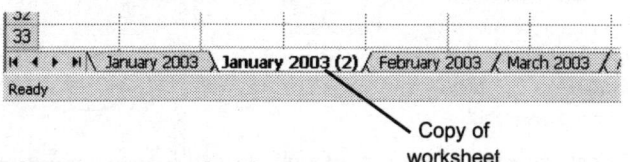

Copy of worksheet

Delete a worksheet

To delete a worksheet and all its data:

1 Save the file and then click on a sheet tab.

2 From the **Edit** menu, select **Delete Sheet**. You are asked for confirmation that the worksheet is to be deleted.

3 Click on **OK**.

Display several worksheets

You can display several worksheets from the file at the same time.

1 Click on the current worksheet's ▣ button to reduce the size of the worksheet window within the main Excel window.

2 From the **Window** menu, select **New Window**. Two overlapping windows are now displayed.

3 Rearrange the windows by selecting **Arrange** from the **Window** menu and choosing a suitable option.

You can now move around in either window and display data from different worksheets (or display two parts of the same worksheet).

You can close any of the windows by clicking on their ✖ buttons.

You can make the windows fill the Excel window again by clicking on the ▣ button on the current worksheet window. You can then switch between the open windows using the numbered options at the bottom of the **Window** menu.

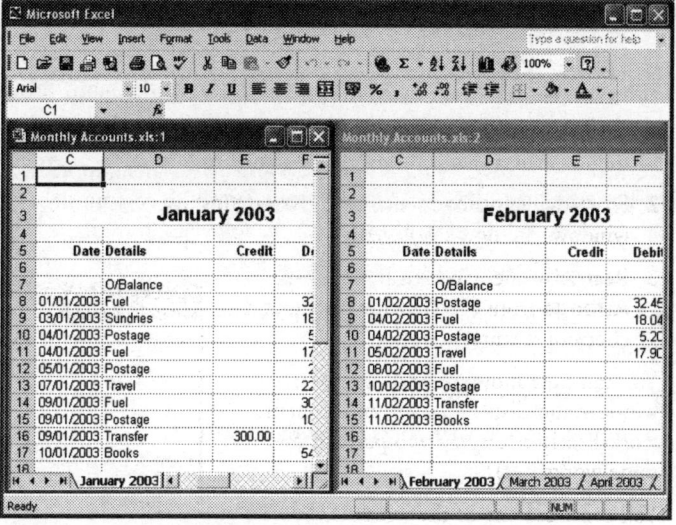

WINDOWS ARRANGED VERTICALLY

Open several files

You can also display windows on worksheets from more than one file at a time. Selecting **Open** from the **File** menu opens a file in a new window. You can switch between any of the open windows using the options in the **Window** menu.

Refer to cells from another worksheet

A formula can refer to a cell or range in another worksheet. The reference is preceded by the sheet name and an exclamation mark (!). For example, cell G7 in Sheet2 may be made to contain the same value as cell G30 in Sheet1 with the following formula:

= Sheet1!G30

If the sheet name contains spaces, it must be enclosed in single quotes. For example:

= 'January 2003'!G30

To create a formula that refers to another sheet:

1 Open two windows, rearrange them inside the Excel window and display the two relevant worksheets in them.

2 Click on the sheet that is to contain the formula; click on the cell where you want the formula.

3 Type the formula up to the point where the reference is required.

4 Click on the other worksheet; click on the cell or mark the range that is needed for the formula. The reference (including sheet name) is added to the formula.

5 Finish typing the formula.

Create ranges over multiple worksheets

A formula can refer to a range that covers more than one worksheet. The formula must specify the first and last worksheets to be covered by the range, separated by colons. For example:

= SUM(Sheet1:Sheet12!E8:E30)

This formula gives you the total of the values in the range E8:E30 over all sheets between Sheet1 and Sheet12.

If the sheet names include spaces, everything to the left of the exclamation mark must be contained in single quotes:

= SUM('January 2003:December 2003'!E8:E30)

In this case the ranges are totalled over all sheets between those named 'January 2003' and 'December 2003' inclusive.

The sheets included are those whose tabs lie between the specified sheet tabs. So the data on 'February 2003' will only be included if this sheet lies between the other two; if you move the sheet to the left of 'January 2003', the data will no longer be added into the total.

Refer to cells from another file

A formula can refer to a cell or range in another workbook. The filename is included in the reference, immediately before the sheet name, in square brackets. For example:

= '[Monthly Accounts.xls]January 2003'!G7

The result of this formula is updated whenever you open the file.

To create a formula that refers to another file:

1 Open two windows, one for each file.

2 Enter the formula up to the point at which the formula is required.

3 Click on the other file's window; click on the cell or mark the range required.

4 Finish typing the formula.

tip

If you cut-and-paste a formula from one file to another, any references to cells on the same sheet will be updated to refer to the same relative cells in the new file, in the usual way. However, references to cells on another sheet (in the same file) will be updated to include the original filename in the copied formula. Therefore you may need to edit out these file references.

Copy data and formulae between worksheets

You can copy the contents of any cell or range from one worksheet to another.

1 Click on the cell or mark the range to be copied. Press **[Ctrl] + [C]**.

2 Click on the second sheet.

3 Click on the cell where the copy is to be made. Press **[Ctrl] + [V]**.

Copy formatting between worksheets

To copy the display format to a cell on another worksheet:

1 Click on a cell whose display format you want to duplicate.

2 Click on the button on the toolbar.

3 Click on the second sheet.

4 Click on a cell or mark a range.

12

lists

Add a list

Excel provides options for handling record-based data, where each record has the same layout. Such data is stored in a list.

1 Start a new worksheet.

2 Enter a series of labels in a row on the worksheet. You can start at any cell but there must be no empty cells within the series.

3 Mark a range covering the labels.

4 From the **Format** menu, select **Cells** and click on the **Text** category. Click on **OK**.

5 Change the text font or attributes. (There must be a difference in format between the labels and records.)

6 Enter any required formulae on the row below the labels and copy them to the following three rows.

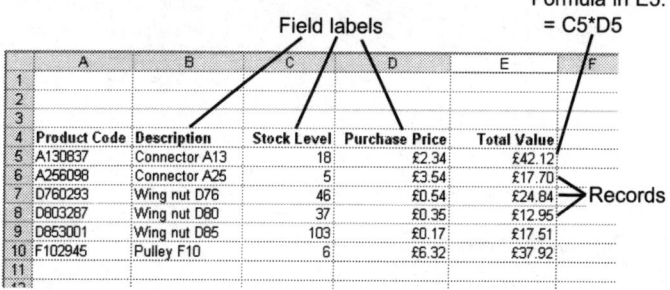

Field labels

Formula in E5:
= C5*D5

	A	B	C	D	E	F
1						
2						
3						
4	Product Code	Description	Stock Level	Purchase Price	Total Value	
5	A130837	Connector A13	18	£2.34	£42.12	
6	A256098	Connector A25	5	£3.54	£17.70	
7	D760293	Wing nut D76	46	£0.54	£24.84	→ Records
8	D803287	Wing nut D80	37	£0.35	£12.95	
9	D853001	Wing nut D85	103	£0.17	£17.51	
10	F102945	Pulley F10	6	£6.32	£37.92	
11						

Add a record using a data form

Data forms provide a means of adding, editing and deleting records in a list. (You can also add records directly – see page 174.)

1 Click on a cell within the list.

2 From the **Data** menu, select **Form**. The data form is displayed and shows the first record in the list.

Number of records in list

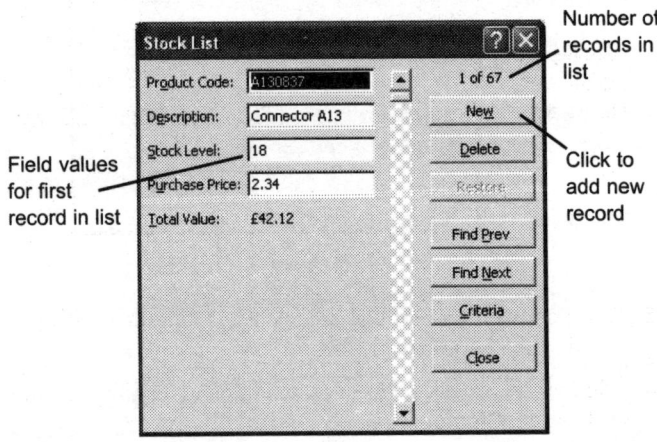

Field values for first record in list

Click to add new record

3 Click on the **New** button.

4 Type a value in each of the fields. Click on **[Tab]** to move from one field to the next.

Enter values for new record

Formula will be calculated

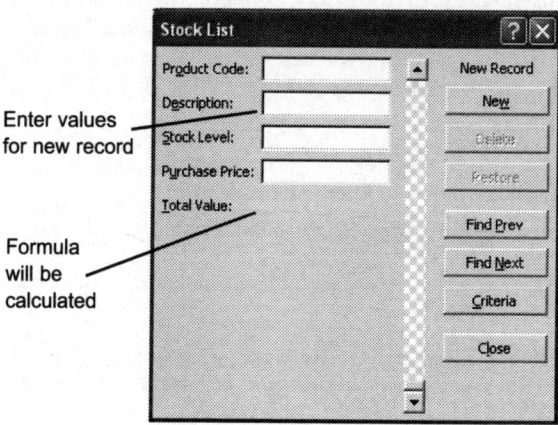

5 Press **[Enter]**. Any formulae are calculated and the record is added to the bottom of the list.

6 Add another record, perform an action on an existing record or click on the **Close** button.

Add records directly

You can add records directly to the worksheet. When you type in the data for a new record (at the bottom of the list), the formulae are automatically copied from the row above. There must be no blank rows between records.

You can also add other data to the worksheet but this must be above or below the list (not to the left or right) and must be separated from the list by at least one blank row.

tip

To insert a record in the middle of the list, insert a new row in the usual way and then type the values directly into the cells or use the data form to edit the new, blank record.

Edit a record using a data form

To edit a record:

1 Click on a cell within the list.

2 From the **Data** menu, select **Form**.

3 Find the record to be edited by dragging the scroll bar in the middle of the dialog box.

4 Click on any field and edit or retype the value.

5 Press **[Enter]**.

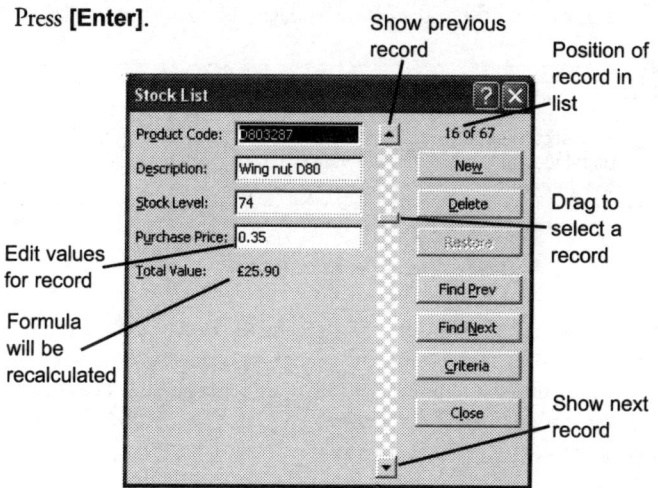

Show previous record

Position of record in list

Edit values for record

Formula will be recalculated

Drag to select a record

Show next record

Stock List

Product Code: D803287

Description: Wing nut D80

Stock Level: 74

Purchase Price: 0.35

Total Value: £25.90

16 of 67

New

Delete

Restore

Find Prev

Find Next

Criteria

Close

Delete a record using a data form

To delete a record:

1 Click on a cell within the list.

2 From the **Data** menu, select **Form**.

3 Find the record to be deleted by dragging the scroll bar in the middle of the dialog box.

4 Click on the **Delete** button.

5 Confirm that the record is to be deleted by clicking on **OK**.

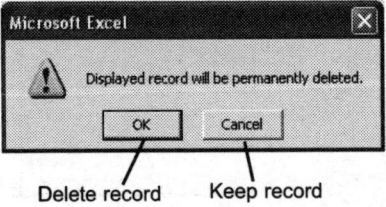

Delete record   Keep record

The record numbers in the top right-hand corner of the data form are allocated by the system and cannot be changed. When you delete records, the remaining records are renumbered. Therefore the number for any particular record may change as records are added and deleted.

Find a record using a data form

You can find any records that satisfy given conditions.

1 Click on a cell within the list.

2 From the **Data** menu, select **Form**.

3 Click on the **Criteria** button.

4 Enter values or conditions in the fields (see below).

5 Click on **Find Next** to find the next record that matches all the criteria or **Find Prev** for the previous matching record.

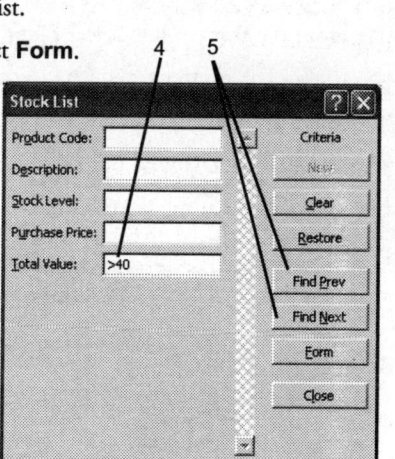

Each of the criteria can be one of the following:

• An exact value to be matched

• The first few characters of a text field

• A comparison operator (>, >=, <, <= or <>) and value (e.g. >40 if the value must be greater than 40)

Filter a list

The AutoFilter feature allows you to hide records that do not match given criteria.

1 From the **Data** menu, select **Filter** and then **AutoFilter**.

2 Right-click on the arrow next to the field name.

3 Select a value, click on **(Top 10...)** to choose the records with the highest or lowest values, or click on **(Custom...)** to devise a condition based on field values.

Product Coc ▾	Description ▾	Stock Lev ▾	Purchase Pri ▾	Total Valu ▾
A130837	Connector A13	(All)	£2.34	£42.12
A256098	Connector A25	(Top 10...)	£3.54	£17.70
D760293	Wing nut D76	(Custom...)	£0.54	£24.84
D803287	Wing nut D80	2	£0.35	£12.95
D853001	Wing nut D85	3	£0.17	£17.51
F102945	Pulley F10	4	£6.32	£37.92
F112976	Pulley F11	5	£7.45	£29.80
F204396	Belt (2m)	6	£1.80	£21.60
F214396	Belt (2.4m)	7	£1.96	£19.60
F379366	Spindle F37	8	£18.45	£36.90
		9		
		10		
		12		

4 The list shows only matching records. The arrows next to the fields with conditions attached are shown in blue.

To restore the full list: from the **Data** menu, select **Filter** and then **AutoFilter** again.

13

charts and graphics

Create a chart

Excel's Chart Wizard allows you to create a chart or graph to illustrate your data.

1 Mark the range of data, including any appropriate labels above and to the left of the main block of data.

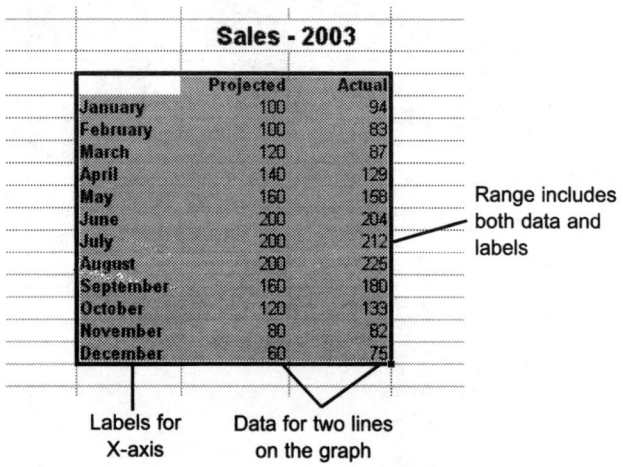

Sales - 2003

	Projected	Actual
January	100	94
February	100	83
March	120	87
April	140	129
May	160	158
June	200	204
July	200	212
August	200	225
September	160	180
October	120	139
November	80	82
December	60	75

Range includes both data and labels

Labels for X-axis   Data for two lines on the graph

2 Click on the 🏛 button.

Chart Wizard   100%

3 Click on a **Chart type** and then on one of the **Chart sub-type** boxes. Click on **Next**.

Design your own
chart type

For selected chart
type, choose sub-type

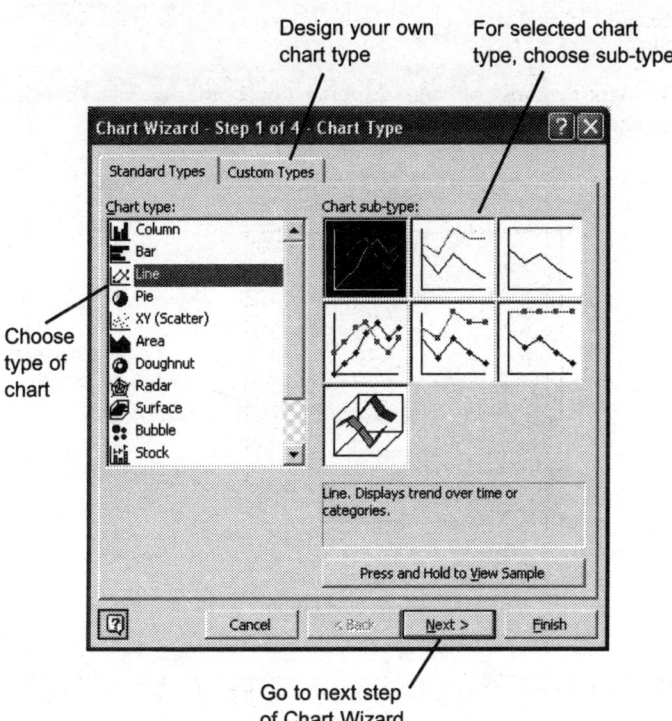

Choose
type of
chart

Go to next step
of Chart Wizard

4 Check that the correct range of data has been selected and that the series have been correctly identified. (Click on **Rows** if each line on the graph is to represent the data in a row rather than a column.) Click on **Next**.

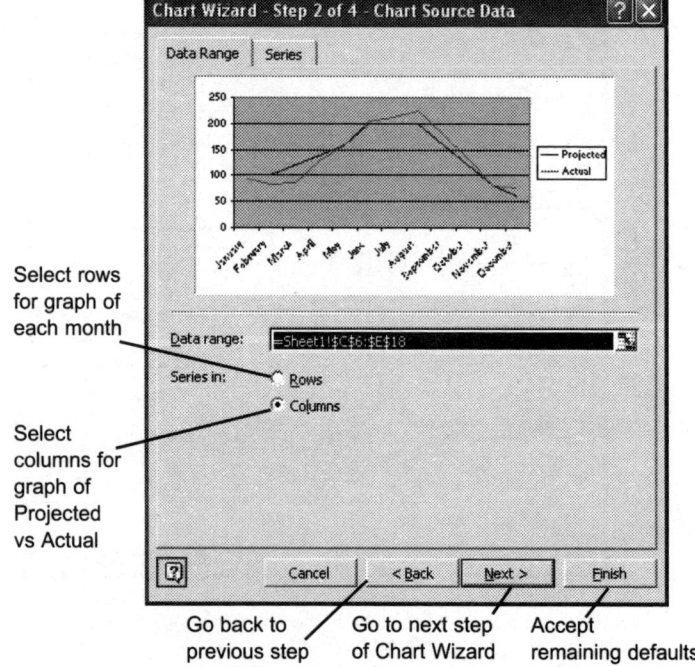

Select rows for graph of each month

Select columns for graph of Projected vs Actual

Go back to previous step

Go to next step of Chart Wizard

Accept remaining defaults

5 Enter a title for the chart and labels for the axes. Click on **Next**.

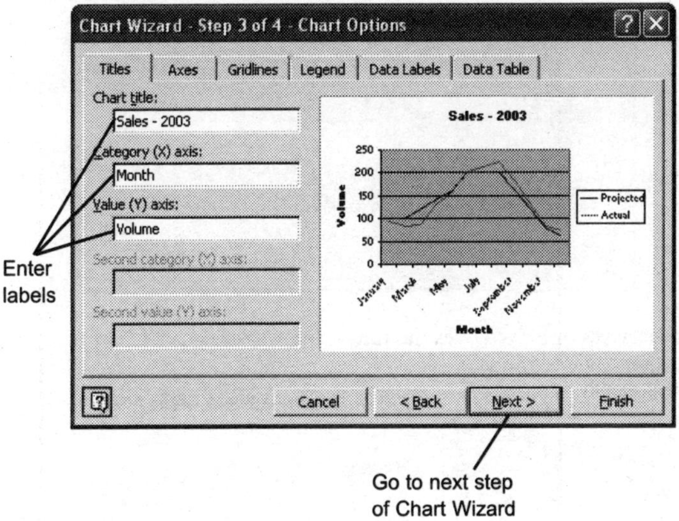

Chart Wizard - Step 3 of 4 - Chart Options   ? ✕

Titles | Axes | Gridlines | Legend | Data Labels | Data Table

Chart title:
Sales - 2003

Category (X) axis:
Month

Value (Y) axis:
Volume

Second category (X) axis:

Second value (Y) axis:

Sales - 2003

—— Projected
······ Actual

Volume

Month

Enter
labels

                Cancel | < Back | Next > | Finish

Go to next step
of Chart Wizard

tip

You can change other features of the graph, such as the display
of grid lines or a legend, by clicking on the other tabs. These
features can also be altered when the chart is complete (see
page 186).

6 Choose where you want to place the chart: as a separate chart sheet in the workbook or in one of the existing worksheets. Click on **Finish**.

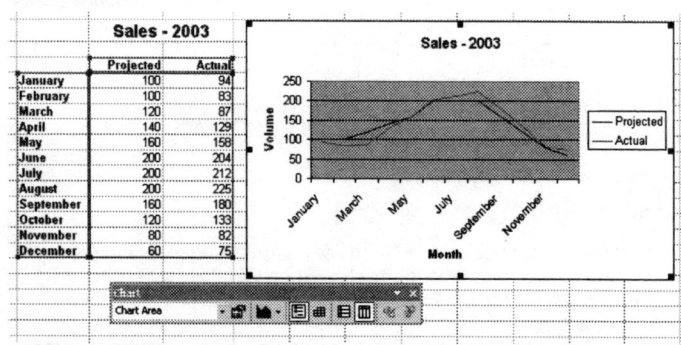

A chart is displayed over the top of the worksheet. A Chart toolbar is also shown.

Change the chart size and position

The size and position of a chart can be modified.

To change the size and position of the chart:

- Drag the chart to any position on the sheet. The contents of the cells underneath the chart are not affected.

- Change the size of the chart by clicking on it and then dragging the sizing handles on the sides and corners.

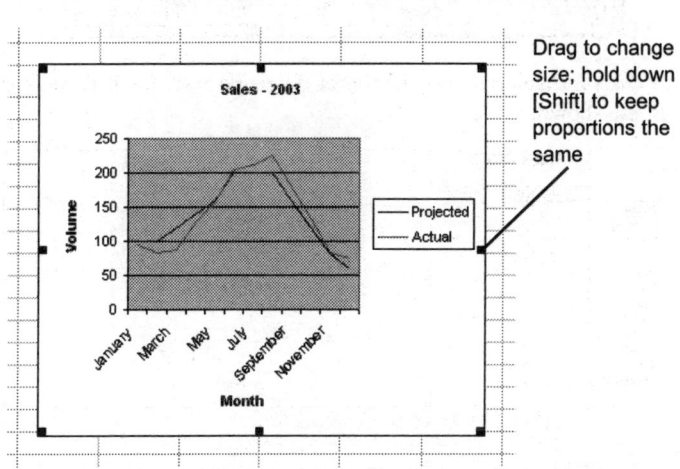

Drag to change size; hold down [Shift] to keep proportions the same

Change the chart appearance

You can change the appearance of many individual features in a chart (such as the axes, labels and background). These changes can be made to charts overlaid on worksheets or separate chart sheets.

To change the chart features:

1 Move the pointer over the chart. A pop-up label tells you which feature you are pointing to.

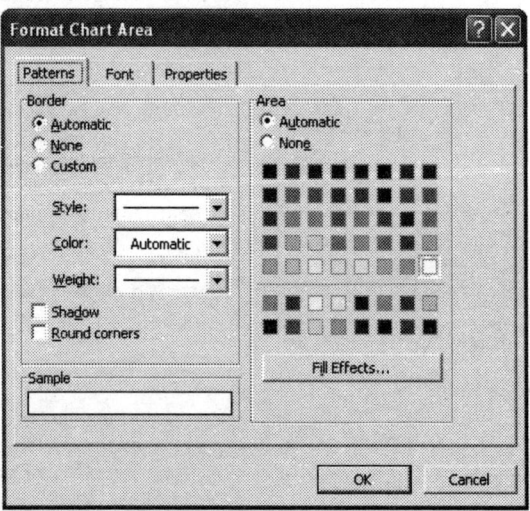

Dialog displayed after clicking on blank area of chart

2 Double-click on the feature to be changed.

3 The relevant dialog box is displayed. Make the required changes on each of the tabs.

4 Click on **OK**.

Or

1 In the Chart toolbar, select the feature from the **Chart Objects** box.

2 Click on the required button for the type of change to be made.

3 Make the changes in the dialog box.

4 Click on **OK**.

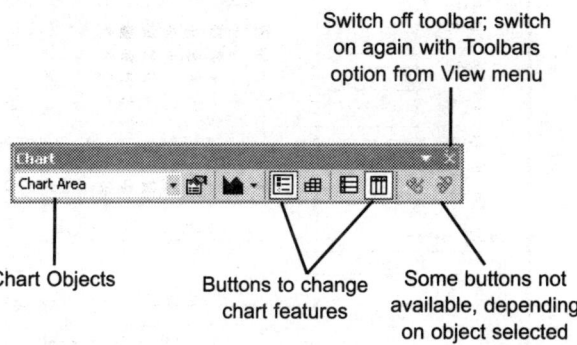

Switch off toolbar; switch on again with Toolbars option from View menu

Chart Objects

Buttons to change chart features

Some buttons not available, depending on object selected

Change the data shown in a chart

The range of data illustrated in the chart can be expanded or reduced without creating a new chart.

1 Right-click on the graph area of the chart and select **Source Data**.

2 In the **Data Range** tab, change the data to be graphed either by editing the value in the **Data range** box or by marking a new range in the sheet.

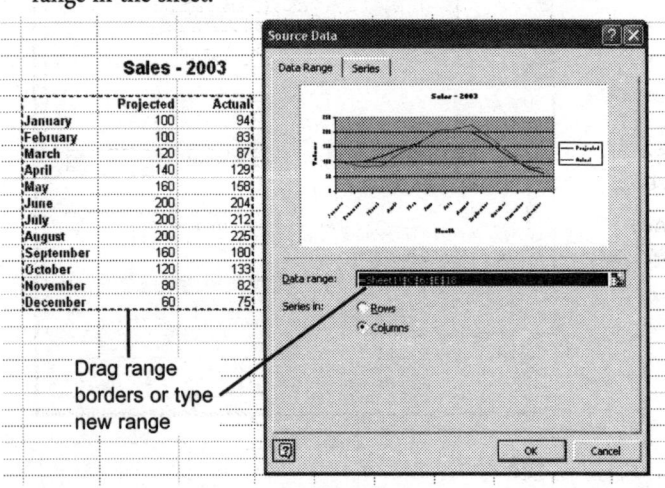

Drag range borders or type new range

3 In the **Series** tab, add or remove data series and their labels as required.

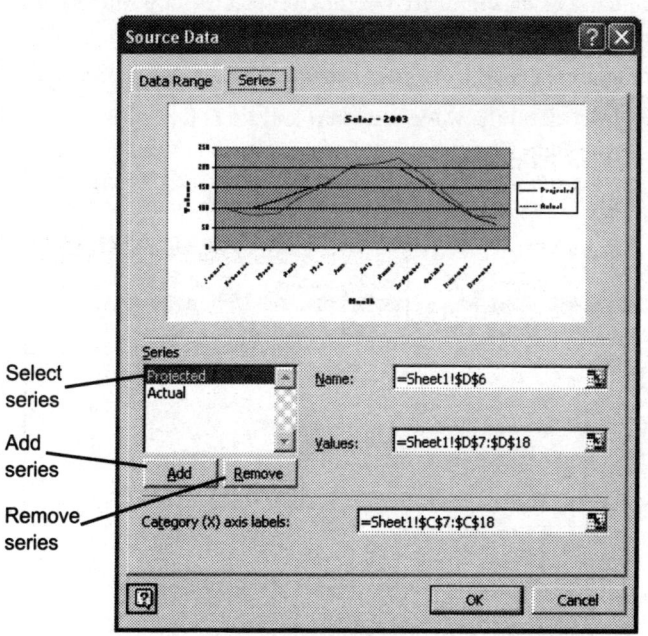

Select series

Add series

Remove series

4 Click on **OK**.

Create a chart sheet

The final stage of the Chart Wizard gives you the opportunity to create a separate sheet for the chart.

You can also convert a worksheet chart to a chart sheet.

1 Right-click on the worksheet chart and select **Location**.

2 Click on **As new sheet**.

3 Replace 'Chart1' with a suitable name for the chart sheet.

4 Click on **OK**.

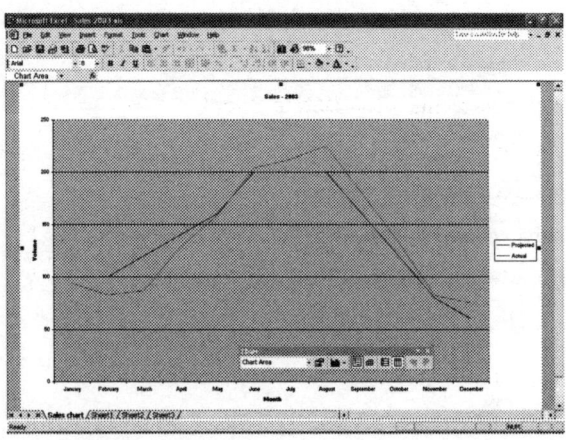

Create a chart quickly

To create a chart using all the Excel defaults:

1 Mark the range of data to be illustrated, including appropriate labels.

2 Press function key **[F11]**. The chart is displayed immediately and can be edited (see page 186).

Delete a chart

To remove a chart sheet from the workbook:

1 Click on the sheet tab for the chart.

2 From the **Edit** menu, select **Delete Sheet**.

3 Click on **OK**.

To remove a chart from a worksheet:

1 Click on a white area of the chart.

2 Press **[Delete]**.

Use the Drawing toolbar

You can add pictures, graphics and text boxes to your worksheet using the Drawing toolbar.

- To show the Drawing toolbar, click on the 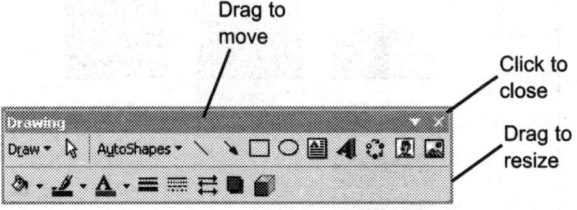 button on the toolbar.

- Initially, the toolbar is 'docked' at the bottom of the window. You can change it into a 'floating' toolbar by dragging the vertical bar on the left of the toolbar into the middle of the window.

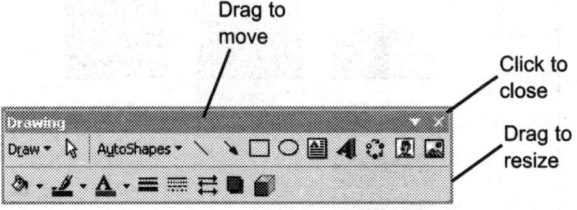

- To move a floating toolbar, drag the title bar.

- To change the dimensions of the toolbar, drag the edges.

- To hide the toolbar, click on the 🎨 button again or click on the toolbar's ✖ button.

Add a picture

You can add any picture to the worksheet, providing it is stored in a file in a standard picture format.

1 From the **Insert** menu, select **Picture** and **From File** (or click on the 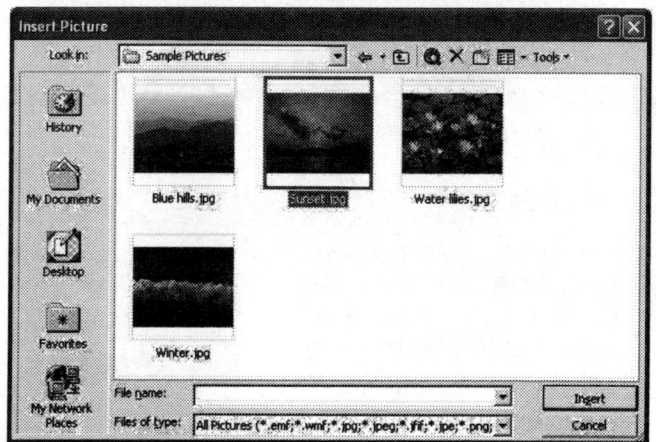 button).

2 Choose a file from the dialog box and click on **Insert**.

You can also click on the button to insert a standard ClipArt file (or add your own pictures to the ClipArt Gallery).

Add a graphic object

The Drawing toolbar includes several objects that can be included on a worksheet.

To add a rectangle or oval:

1 Click on the appropriate button on the Drawing toolbar.

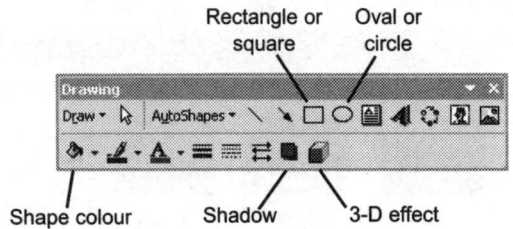

Rectangle or square   Oval or circle

Shape colour   Shadow   3-D effect

2 Mark out the area to be covered by the object by dragging the pointer. To add a square or circle, hold down the **[Shift]** key as you drag.

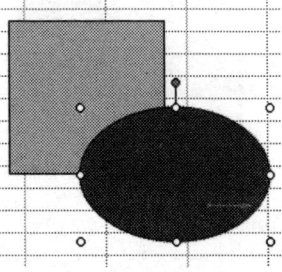

3 Click on the 🖎 button to set the colour of the object.

4 Click on the arrow to the right of the 🖎 button to select a new colour.

5 Click on the appropriate buttons to add a shadow or 3-D effect.

To add a line or arrow:

1 Click on the appropriate button on the Drawing toolbar.

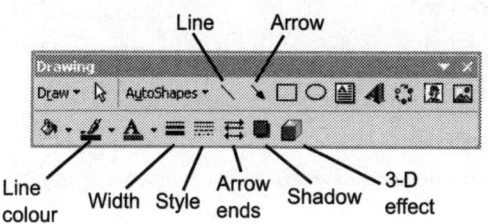

2 Drag the pointer from the start of the line to the end. To add a line at an angle that is a multiple of 15 degrees, hold down the **[Shift]** key as you drag.

3 Click on the ✎ button to set the colour of the line or arrow. Click on the arrow to the right of the button to select a new colour.

4 Click on the appropriate buttons to change the line width, line style or arrow ends, or to add a shadow or 3-D effect.

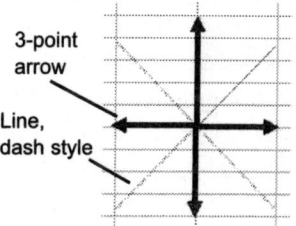

Change a graphic object

Graphic objects (rectangles, ovals, lines and arrows) can be moved, changed, resized or deleted. To move an object:

1 Click on the object.

2 Click inside the object and then drag it to its new position.

To change the appearance of an object:

1 Click on the object.

2 Use the buttons on the Drawing toolbar to choose a new colour, line style etc.

To resize an object:

1 Click on the object.

2 Drag the sizing handles on the edges or corners of the object to change the size. Hold down the **[Shift]** key as you drag to keep the proportions the same.

To delete an object:

1 Click on the object.

2 Press **[Delete]**.

Rotate an object

To rotate an object:

1 Click on the object.

2 Move the mouse pointer to the green circle attached to one of the sizing handles and drag it to right or left.

Add an AutoShape

Excel provides a large number of other shapes (flowchart shapes, stars, connectors and many more).

1 Click on the **AutoShapes** button, then on a category and shape.

2 Drag the pointer to mark out the area of the shape.

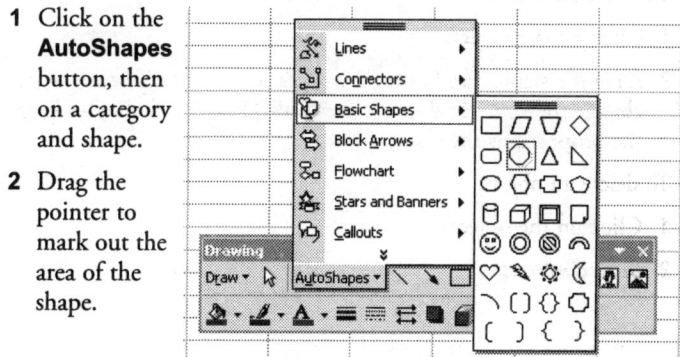

Add a text box

Text boxes allow you to add text for annotations or other additional information to a worksheet. The text box floats over the top of the sheet, so does not affect the underlying cells.

1 Click on the 🖻 button on the Drawing toolbar.

Text box   WordArt

2 Mark the area to be covered by the text box.

3 Type the text.

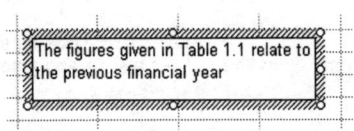

The figures given in Table 1.1 relate to the previous financial year

Change a text box

You can change various features of an existing text box by clicking on it.

- To move a text box, drag it to a new position on the sheet.

- To change the width or height of the box, drag the sizing handles on the edges or corners of the box.

- To change the font, font size or attributes of the text, mark the text and then use the buttons on the Formatting toolbar at the top of the Excel window.

- To change the colour of the text, click on the ⬛ button on either the Drawing toolbar or Formatting toolbar. Click on the arrow to the right of the button to select a new colour.

- To delete a text box, click on the box and press **[Delete]**.

tip

You can also add curved, coloured and rotated text. Click on the WordArt button on the Drawing toolbar, select a style and type the text. Then use the WordArt toolbar to change the appearance of the text.

14

printing

Change the page size and layout

A worksheet can be printed on paper of any size.

1 From the **File** menu, select **Page Setup**.
2 Click on the **Page** tab.
3 Choose the required **Paper size** from the drop-down list.
4 Select either **Portrait** (tall, thin) or **Landscape** (short, wide).
5 Click on **OK**.

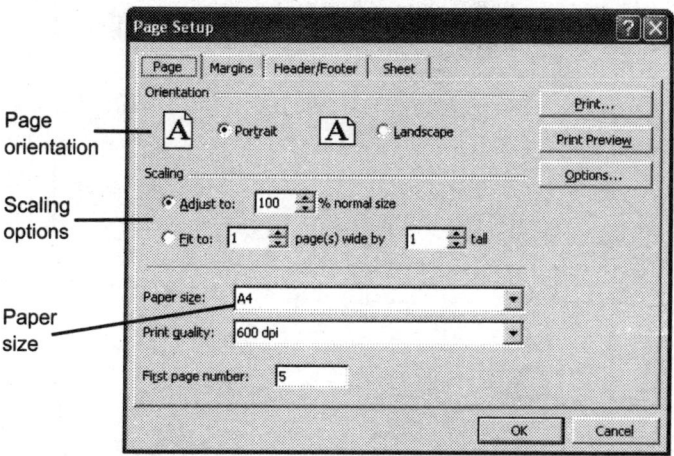

Page orientation

Scaling options

Paper size

Alter the margins

The **Margins** tab on the Page Setup dialog box changes the space around the outside of the printout.

1 From the **File** menu, select **Page Setup**.

2 Click on the **Margins** tab.

3 Enter the size of the top, bottom, left and right margins. The top and bottom margins include the space used by the header and footer respectively.

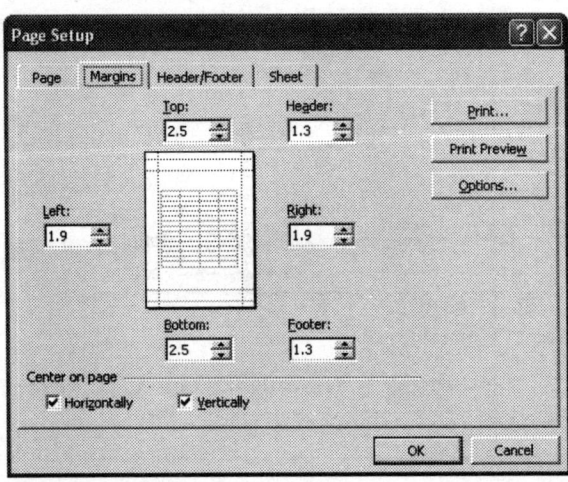

4 Set the distance of the top of the header and the bottom of the footer from the edge of the paper. Make sure the top and bottom margins are large enough to include these distances plus the height of the text.

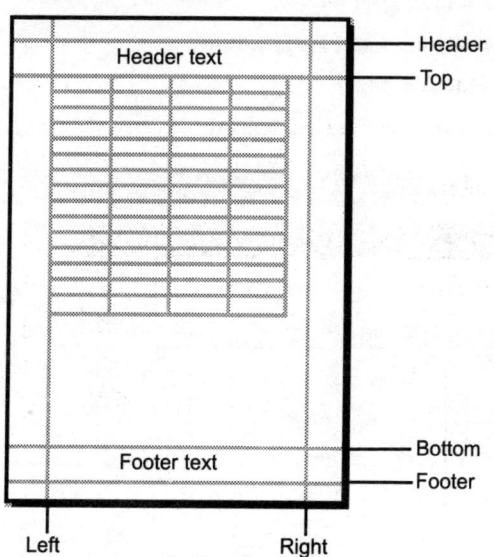

5 Click on **Horizontally** or **Vertically** (or both) to centre the printed worksheet within the print area.

6 Click on **OK**.

Change the header and footer

The header and footer are items of text printed at the top and
bottom of each printed page.

1 From the **File** menu, select **Page Setup**.

2 Click on the **Header/Footer** tab.

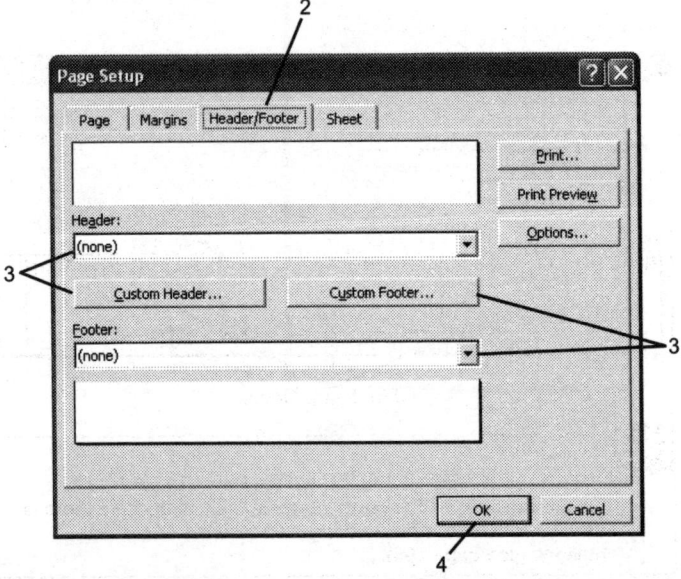

3 Choose a standard header or footer from the drop-down lists.

Or

Click on **Custom Header** or **Custom Footer** to design your own header or footer (see below).

4 Click on **OK**.

Buttons to add codes to header/footer

DIALOG BOX FOR CUSTOM HEADER/FOOTER

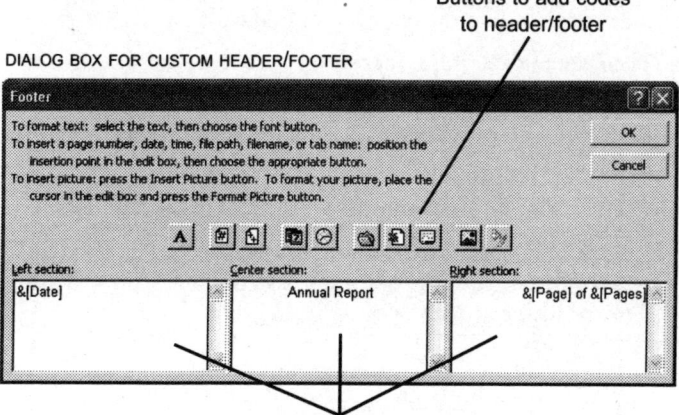

Text for header/footer

tip

If your header or footer covers several lines, make sure there is enough space for it. If necessary, increase the size of the margins (see page 203).

Create a custom header or footer

From the **Header/Footer** tab of the Page Setup dialog box, clicking on **Custom Header** or **Custom Footer** allows you to design your own header or footer.

For a custom header or footer, you can enter your own text and include codes for information relevant to the file:

- There are three sections, for text on the left, centre and right of the page.

- Each item of text can cover several lines; press **[Enter]** to start a new line.

- Click on the **A** button to change the font of selected text.

- Include codes for the date, time, page number etc. by clicking on the relevant buttons. When the page is printed, the codes are replaced by the actual values.

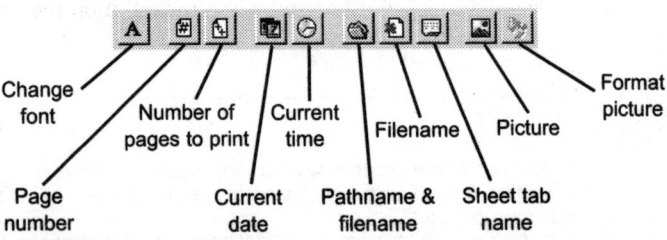

Set the start page number

By default, the first page is page 1. If the printout is to be part of some larger document you can set a different start page number.

1 From the **File** menu, select **Page Setup**.

2 Click on the **Page** tab.

3 Enter a number in the **First page number** box.

4 Click on **OK**.

Remove a header or footer

To print an empty margin at the top or bottom of the page:

1 From the **File** menu, select **Page Setup**.

2 Click on the **Header/Footer** tab.

3 Click on the **Header** or **Footer** box and select '(none)' from the drop-down list.

4 Click on **OK**.

Select the order for printing pages

If a worksheet is too large to print on a single page, it is split over a number of pages. If the worksheet is both too wide and too long for a standard page, it is split both horizontally and vertically. You can decide the order in which the pages are printed.

Repeat borders

Select order for printing

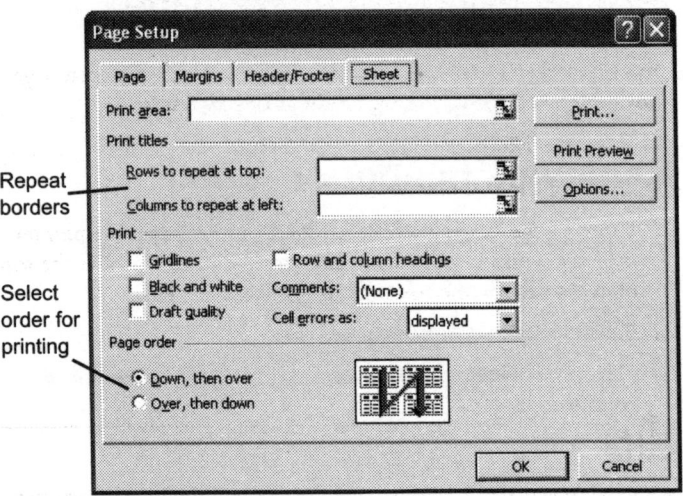

1 From the **File** menu, select **Page Setup**.

2 Click on the **Sheet** tab.

3 Select **Down, then over** if you want to print the pages vertically down the sheet first; select **Over, then down** if you want to print horizontally across the sheet first.

4 Click on **OK**.

Print borders on every page

You can repeat a particular set of rows and columns on each page (for example, a set of column headings or row labels).

1 From the **File** menu, select **Page Setup**.

2 Click on the **Sheet** tab.

3 Click on the appropriate **Print titles** box and drag the pointer over the worksheet, marking either the rows to repeat at the top of every page or the columns to repeat on the left.

4 Click on **OK**.

The effect of repeating borders is similar to that of freezing rows and columns (see page 57).

Print part of a worksheet

To reduce the area of the worksheet that is printed:

1 From the **File** menu, select **Page Setup**.

2 Click on the **Sheet** tab.

3 Click on the **Print area** box and drag the pointer over the worksheet, marking the area that you want printed.

4 Click on **OK**.

Area to be printed —

Repeat borders —

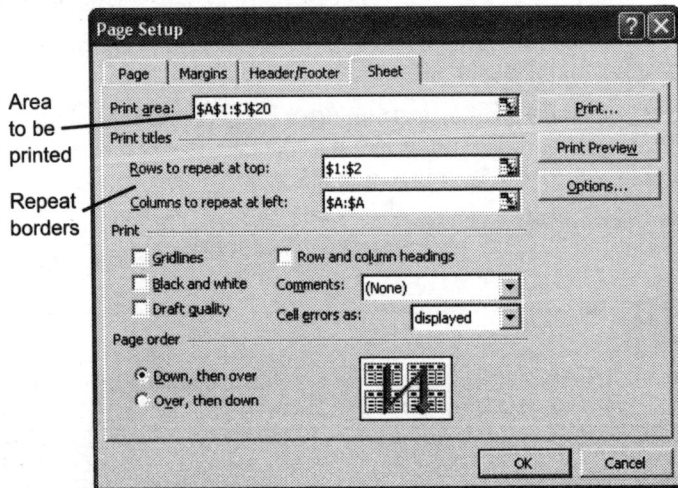

Change other print settings

The **Sheet** tab of the Page Setup dialog box allows you to set the following options:

- Whether or not background grid lines are printed.

- Printing in black and white (if the box is selected) or colour.

- Printing in draft mode (which may be faster) or full quality mode.

- Whether or not the row numbers and column letters are printed.

- Whether comments are printed (see page 218) and, if they are, where on the printout they appear.

Click on the check boxes to select or deselect the items.

Click on box to print row
numbers and column letters

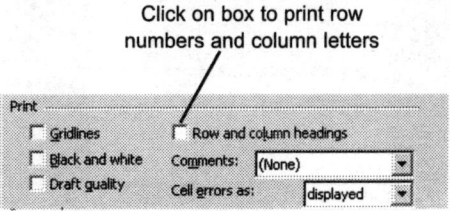

Preview the pages to print

Click on the 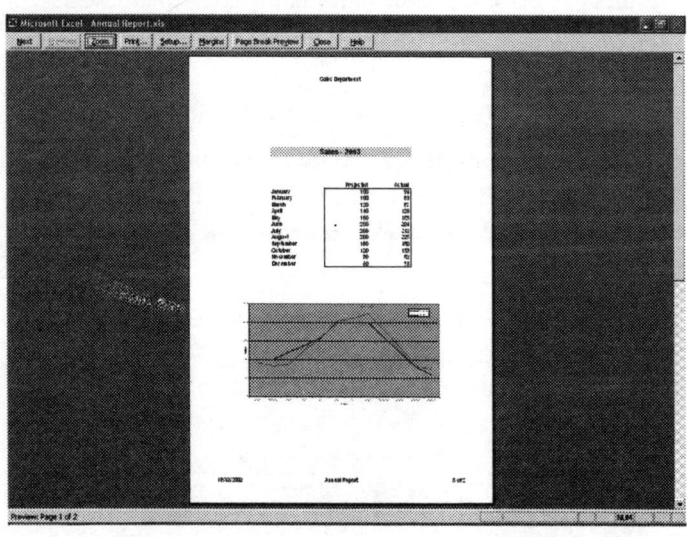 button to see what the worksheet will look like when it is printed. Alternatively, click on the **Print Preview** button in any of the Page Setup tabs.

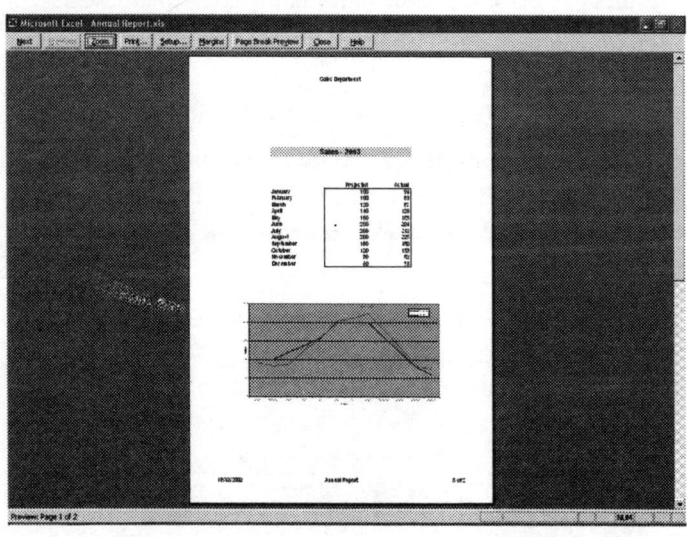

The buttons at the top of the Print Preview window are used as follows:

- Click on **Previous** or **Next** to look at the pages before or after the current page.

- Click on **Zoom** to magnify the preview or show the whole page at once.

- Click on **Print** to start the print process; click on **Setup** to change any of the Print Setup options.

- Click on **Margins** to display the margin settings. Drag any of the margins to adjust them. (The changes will be reflected in the **Margins** tab on the Page Setup dialog box.)

- Click on **Page Break Preview** to change the rows and columns where page breaks occur when printing.

- Click on **Close** to return to normal worksheet view.

- Click on **Help** to display help on the Print Preview window.

Print a worksheet or workbook

To print one or more worksheets from the current workbook:

1 From the **File** menu, select **Print**.

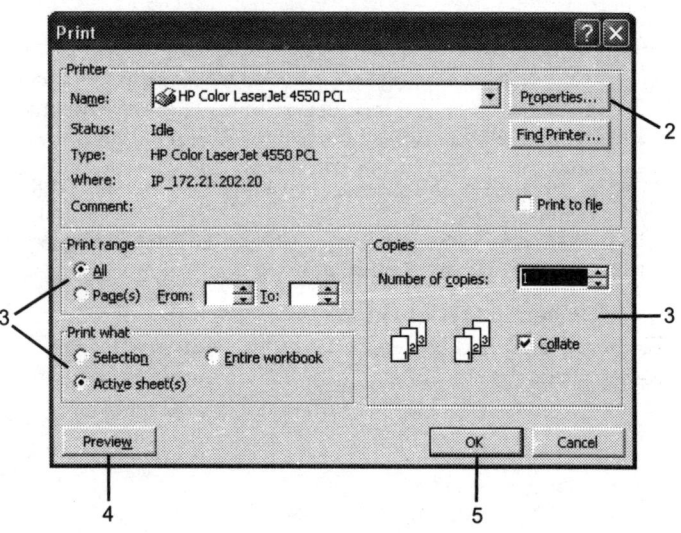

2 Click on the **Properties** button if you want to change the way the printer is set up.

3 Change any of the print defaults, as required (see below).

4 Click on the **Preview** button if you want to see what the printout will look like before you start.

5 Click on **OK**.

You can change the way the sheets are printed as follows:

- In the **Print range** section, click on **All** to print everything. Alternatively, click on **Page(s)** to print only selected pages and enter the first and last page numbers to print. (Use the **Preview** button to see how the worksheet is arranged on the pages.)

- In the **Print what** section, choose between **Selection** (the range that is marked on the current worksheet), **Active sheet(s)** (all sheets whose tabs are currently selected) and **Entire workbook** (all sheets in the current file).

- In the **Copies** section, specify the number of copies to print. For multiple copies, click on **Collate** if you want to print the copies as complete sets (rather than printing multiple copies of each page in turn).

Change the print scaling

The worksheet can be scaled to a particular size or made to fit a specific number of pages.

1 From the **File** menu, select **Page Setup**.

2 Click on the **Page** tab.

3 Click on **Adjust to** and enter the size of the printout as a percentage of its normal size (e.g. 50% to fit into an area half the normal height and width).

Or

Click on **Fit to** to make the worksheet fit a specified number of pages. For example, click on the button but leave both values as 1 to make the printout expand or reduce to fit a single page.

4 Click on **OK**.

Scaling options →

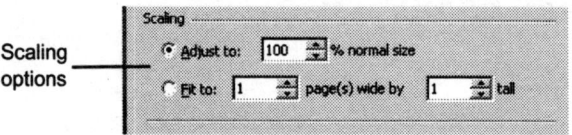

15

enhancing the worksheet

Add a comment

Comments can be attached to cells to annotate them.

1 Right-click on the cell to be annotated and select **Insert Comment**.

2 Type the comment. The text wraps over from one line to the next but you can also press **[Enter]** to start a new line. You can change the name on the first line.

3 Click on another part of the sheet. The cell with the comment now has a small red triangle in the top right-hand corner.

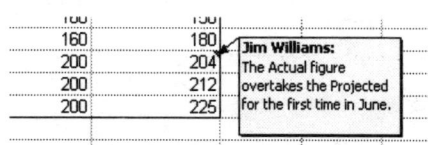

View a comment

To view a comment:

- To view a comment temporarily, move the pointer over the cell. The comment pops up until you move the pointer away.

- To view a comment permanently, right-click on the cell and select **Show Comment**. To hide the comment again, right-click and select **Hide Comment**.

Edit a comment

To edit a comment:

1 Right-click on the cell with the comment and select **Edit Comment**.

2 Make the changes to the comment text.

3 Click on another cell.

Delete a comment

To delete a comment, right-click on the cell and select **Delete Comment**.

Find a cell

You can search a worksheet for cells containing a specific value or item of text.

1 From the **Edit** menu, select **Find** or press **[Ctrl]** + **[F]**.

2 Type the text or value to search for.

3 Click on **Find Next**. The first cell containing the specified text or value is selected. (For example, if you are searching for 'Sept' then any cell containing 'September' or 'transept' is found.)

4 Keep clicking on **Find Next** until you have found the cell you are searching for.

5 Click on **Close**.

Click for
search options

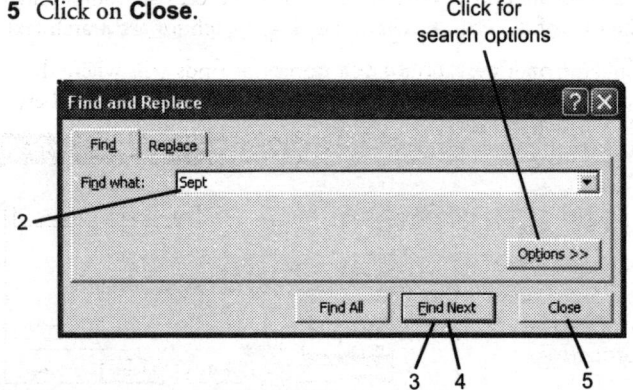

2 —

3   4   5

Modify a search

Click on **Options** to modify the search in the following ways:

- Search within the **Sheet** or the entire **Workbook**.

- By default, the search is performed column-by-column. The **Search** box lets you search row-by-row, so that the cells are found in a different order.

- The **Look in** box lets you choose between searching **Formulas** (both formulae and values are searched), **Values** (only values and the results of formulae are searched) or **Comments** (the search takes place in comments only, not in the cells).

- Clicking on **Match case** has the effect that cells are found only if the case of the cell contents is an exact match for the search text.

- Clicking on **Match entire cell contents** finds cells where the contents are identical to the search text, rather than cells where the contents contain the search text.

- The **Format** button lets you search for cells with particular formatting.

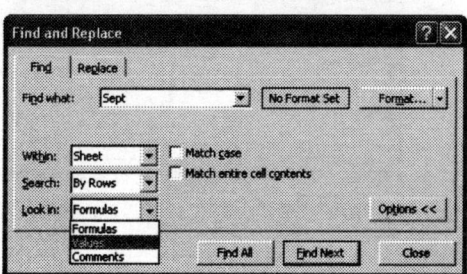

Replace one value with another

You can search a worksheet for a specific value and then replace it
with another value.

1 From the **Edit** menu, select **Replace** or press **[Ctrl] + [H]**.

2 In the **Find what** box, type the text or value to search for.

3 In the **Replace with** box, type the text or value that is to replace
the search value.

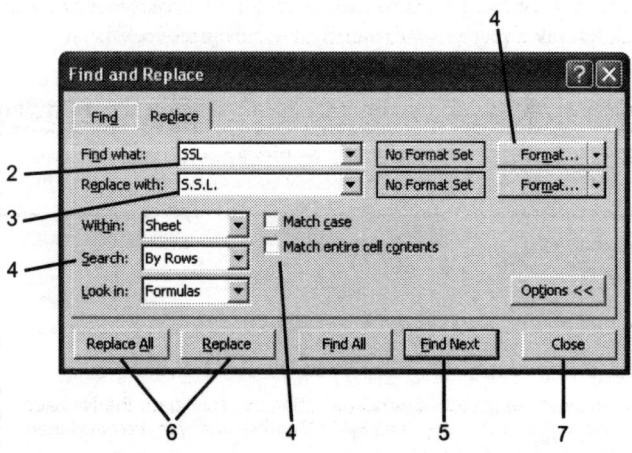

4 As for the **Find** command, clicking on the **Options** button lets you choose where you search, the direction of the search (by rows or columns), whether the case of the text is important and whether to search for partial or exact matches. You can also search for cells with a particular type of formatting and replace them with a different format.

5 Click on **Find Next**. The first cell containing the specified text or value is selected.

6 Click on **Replace** to replace the found value with the new value; **Replace All** to replace all occurrences throughout the worksheet; or **Find Next** to move to the next occurrence without making any change. Repeat until all occurrences have been checked.

Microsoft Excel

Microsoft Excel cannot find the data you're searching for. Check your search options, location and formatting.

OK

7 Click on **Close**.

tip

You can also start the Replace option by clicking on the Replace tab in the Find dialog box. Fill in the 'Replace with' box and then continue as before.

Correct spelling mistakes

The Excel spelling checker searches a worksheet for words that are
not included in its dictionary and gives you the opportunity to
change them. The spelling check includes comments but not
formulae or their results.

1 Make A1 the active cell. (Press **[Ctrl]** + **[Home]** to jump straight
to A1.)

2 From the **Tools** menu, select **Spelling** or click on the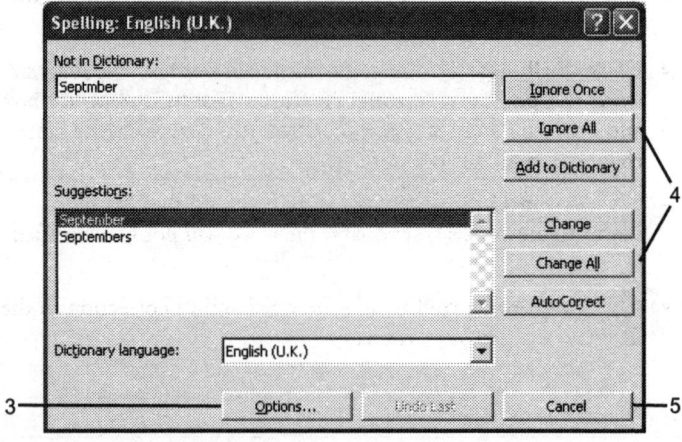
button. The first incorrect spelling is displayed.

Spelling: English (U.K.)

Not in Dictionary:

Septmber — Ignore Once

Ignore All

Add to Dictionary — 4

Suggestions:

September — Change
Septembers

Change All — 4

AutoCorrect

Dictionary language: English (U.K.)

3 — Options...   Undo Last   Cancel — 5

3 If necessary change the way the spelling check is carried out (see page 226).

4 Decide how to handle the word that has been found (see below). Each possible error is displayed in turn.

5 Continue with the spelling check until all words have been checked or stop at any time by clicking on **Cancel**. (You can also cancel the previous change you made by clicking on **Undo Last**.)

For each possible error that is identified, you have the following options:

- Click on **Ignore Once** to jump to the next error or **Ignore All** to ignore all future occurrences of this spelling.

- Click on **Change** to change the incorrect word for the suggested word or type your own correction in the **Not in Dictionary** box and click on **Change**. Click on **Change All** to make the same change throughout the worksheet.

- Click on **Add to Dictionary** to add the word that has been found to the custom dictionary; the word will not be identified in future.

- Click on **AutoCorrect** to add the word and its correction to the AutoCorrect list (see page 227).

Modify the spelling checker

The way the spelling check works can be changed by clicking on the **Options** button, as follows:

- Click on **Suggest from main dictionary only** to decide whether to use an additional *custom* dictionary.

- Click on **Ignore words in UPPERCASE** to ignore any words entirely in capital letters. In a similar way, choose whether to ignore numbers and Internet addresses.

- Select the language for the spelling checker from the **Dictionary language** box.

- In the **Add words to** box, select the name of the file to contain the custom dictionary. Words from this file are assumed to be correct. To start a new dictionary, type a new filename.

Check the spelling in a formula

To check the spelling in a formula:

1 Click on the cell containing the formula.

2 Click on the formula bar.

3 Click on the button.

Make corrections automatically as you type

Excel provides a feature whereby common errors can be corrected as you make entries in the worksheet. The way the corrections are made can be viewed and changed by selecting **AutoCorrect Options** from the **Tools** menu.

The top option determines whether a warning symbol is placed near cells that have been automatically corrected.

The next four options make changes to capital letters as they are entered. Click on **Exceptions** to change the way these options work.

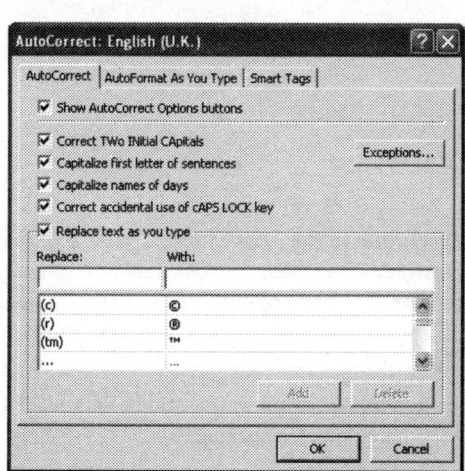

The bottom half of the dialog box lists words that are automatically changed. You can add new words to the list.

Sort a column

The contents of a column or range can be sorted into alphabetical order.

1 Mark part of a column or a range.

2 Click on the ⬆ button to sort the range into ascending (A to Z) order.

Or

Click on the ⬇ button to sort into descending (Z to A) order.

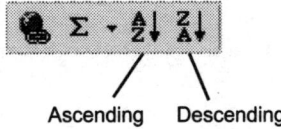

Ascending   Descending

Everything in the marked area is sorted; nothing outside the area is changed. If you have marked a range containing more than one column, the first column is sorted and the values in the other columns move with the sorted values (so that the contents of each row remain the same).

To sort on a column in the middle of a block of data, use the Data Sort dialog box (see page 230).

The values are sorted according to the following rules:

- Values that have a number format all appear above text cells (which includes numbers formatted as text).

- Numbers are sorted into strict numerical order.

- Text is sorted alphabetically, with numbers sorted before letters, capital letters ignored and other symbols sorted according to their ASCII values.

Unsorted	Sorted
2.5	2.5
2000	3
3	25
beta	(no)
25	2000
Gamma	305
305	A1
Alpha	Alpha
(no)	beta
A1	Gamma

If you have chosen to sort into descending order, the sort order is reversed.

Sort on several columns

The contents of a range can be sorted according to the contents of
a column in the middle of the range or according to the contents of
two or three columns.

1 Mark the range to be sorted. All cells in this range will be sorted;
   no cells outside the range will be affected.

2 From the **Data** menu, select **Sort**.

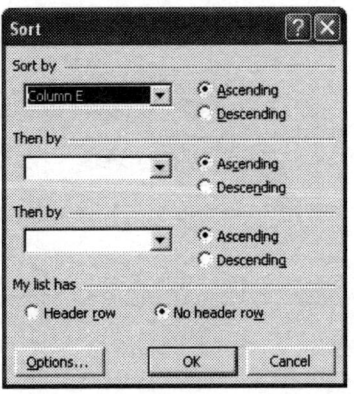

3 Choose the first column on which the sort is to be based. Decide
   whether the sort is to be in ascending or descending order.

4 If required, choose one or two other columns to refine the sort. These can be to the left or right of the first column. If two cells in the first column have the same value, the sort order is determined by the entries in the second column; if these are also the same, the third column is used.

5 If the first row of the marked range includes column labels that are to stay at the top of the columns, click on **Header row**.

6 Click on the **Options** button to make further changes to the way the sort is performed. Click on **OK** after setting the options.

Change the sort order if days of the week or months are to be sorted into chronological rather than alphabetical order

Click to sort lower case letters before capitals

Click to sort along the rows rather than down the columns

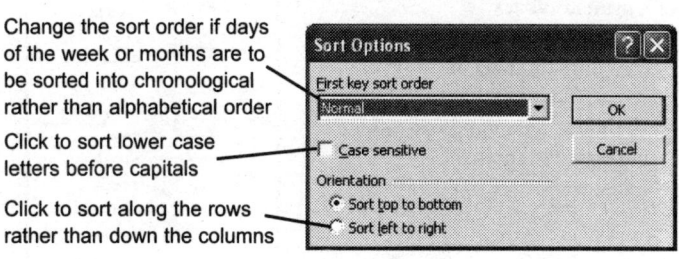

7 Click on **OK** to sort the data.

Display and hide toolbars

Excel is supplied with a number of toolbars, containing buttons for
performing a variety of tasks.

- To display a toolbar,
  from the **View** menu
  select **Toolbars** and
  then click on the
  required toolbar.

- To hide a toolbar, click
  on the toolbar's ✕
  button (if it is a
  'floating' toolbar) or
  select **Toolbars** from
  the **View** menu and
  click on the toolbar
  name again.

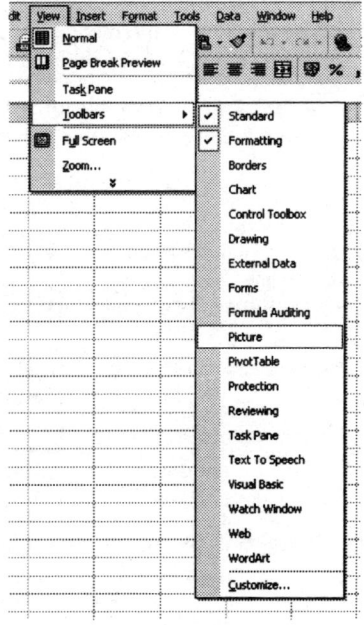

Move a toolbar

Toolbars can be either 'docked' (where they are in a fixed position next to one edge of the Excel window) or 'floating' (where they appear as separate windows within the main Excel window).

- To change a docked toolbar into a floating toolbar, drag the vertical bar on the left-hand side of the toolbar into the middle of the Excel window. Floating toolbars can be moved by dragging their title bars.

- To change a floating toolbar into a docked toolbar, drag the title bar to any edge of the Excel window.

Show more buttons on a toolbar

When several toolbars are docked, there may not be enough room to display all the buttons on the toolbar. You can change the buttons that are shown.

1 Click on the downward-pointing arrow on the right of the toolbar and then click on **Add or Remove Buttons**.

2 Click on individual buttons to add or remove them.

Create a toolbar

New toolbars can be created to group together those buttons that you use most frequently.

1 From the **View** menu, select **Toolbars** and click on the **Customize** option at the bottom of the list.

2 Click on the **Toolbars** tab.

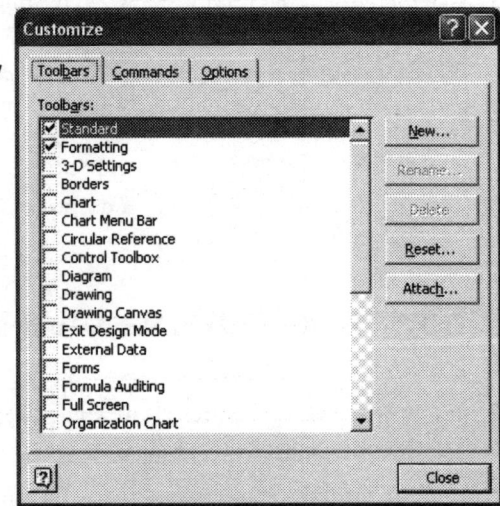

3 Click on the **New** button.

4 Type a name for the toolbar and click on **OK**.

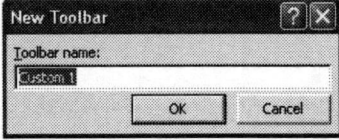

5 Click on the **Commands** tab.

6 Click on an item in the **Categories** list.

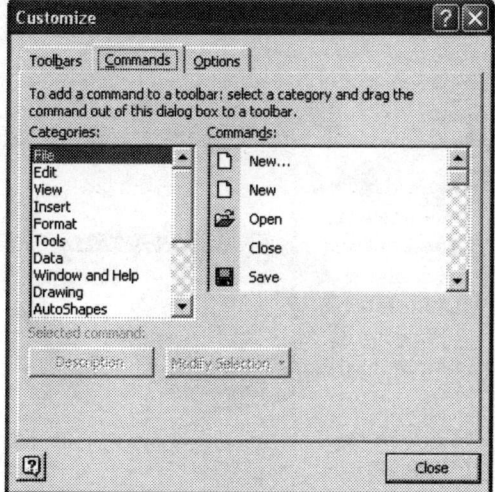

Customize   ? X

Toolbars [Commands] Options

To add a command to a toolbar: select a category and drag the
command out of this dialog box to a toolbar.

Categories: Commands:

File   ▲   🗋 New...   ▲
Edit   🗋 New
View
Insert   🗁 Open
Format
Tools   ▢ Close
Data
Window and Help   💾 Save
Drawing
AutoShapes   ▼   ▼

Selected command:

  Description   Modify Selection ▾

②   Close

7 Drag one or more items from the **Commands** list onto the new toolbar. Repeat for other categories as necessary.

8 Rearrange the selected buttons by dragging them within the new toolbar.

9 Click on **Close**.

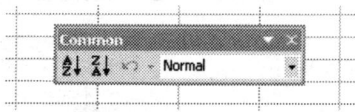

The new toolbar is added to the bottom of the **Toolbars** list.

16

macros

Record a macro

A macro provides a means of automating a series of tasks. A simple macro can be created by recording a sequence of actions.

1 From the **Tools** menu, select **Macro** and **Record New Macro**.

2 Type a name for the macro. The name must consist of letters, numbers and underscore characters, with no spaces.

3 If required, specify a letter for a shortcut. For example, if you type 'M' in the **Shortcut key** box, the macro will be activated whenever you press **[Ctrl] + [M]**.

4 Change the **Description** of the macro so that it describes what the macro actually does.

5 Click on **OK**.

6 A small toolbar appears. Any actions you perform from now on are recorded as part of the macro.

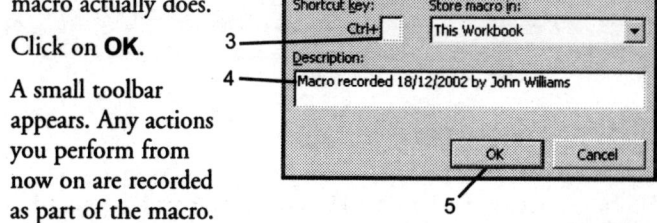

7 Click on the button to finish recording the macro.

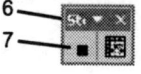

Run a macro

To replay a macro:

1 From the **Tools** menu, select **Macro** and **Macros**.

2 Click on the **Macro name** in the list of macros.

3 Click on the **Run** button.

The sequence of actions is repeated.

If you allocated the macro a shortcut key, you can also run the macro by pressing **[Ctrl]** with the key.

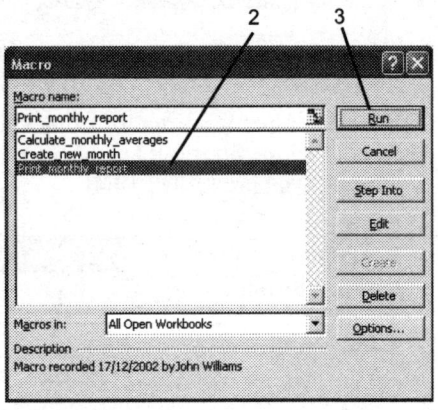

Edit a macro

When you record a macro, Excel converts your actions into a series of Visual Basic instructions. These instructions can be edited.

1 From the **Tools** menu, select **Macro** and **Macros**.

2 Click on the **Macro name** in the list of macros.

3 Click on the **Edit** button. The Visual Basic window is opened, with the macro displayed within it.

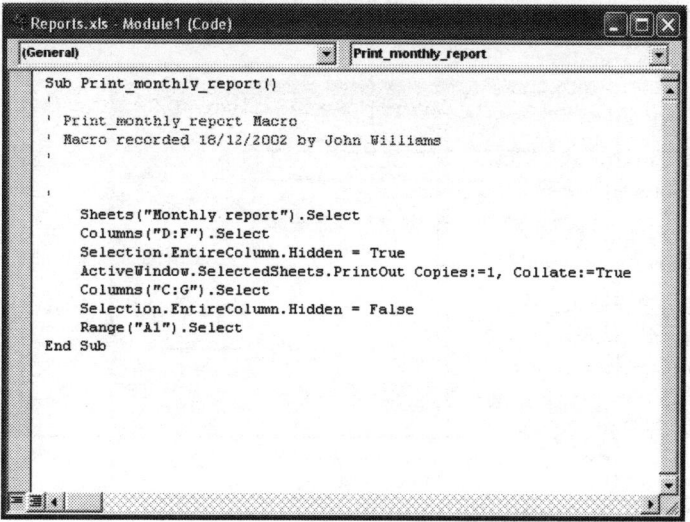

```
Reports.xls - Module1 (Code)

(General)                              Print_monthly_report

    Sub Print_monthly_report()
    '
    ' Print_monthly_report Macro
    ' Macro recorded 18/12/2002 by John Williams
    '

    '
        Sheets("Monthly report").Select
        Columns("D:F").Select
        Selection.EntireColumn.Hidden = True
        ActiveWindow.SelectedSheets.PrintOut Copies:=1, Collate:=True
        Columns("C:G").Select
        Selection.EntireColumn.Hidden = False
        Range("A1").Select
    End Sub
```

4 Make the necessary changes. (See the on-line help for full information on Visual Basic programming.)

5 Close the Visual Basic window.

Use macro options

The Macro dialog box allows you to work with the macros you have created. From the **Tools** menu, select **Macro** and **Macros**; click on a macro name.

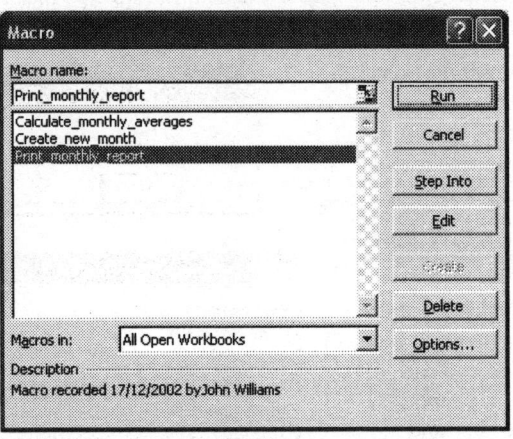

The buttons on the dialog box perform the following operations:

- The **Run** button runs the selected macro (see page 238).

- The **Cancel** button takes you back to the worksheet.

- The **Step Into** button runs the macro one instruction at a time. This is a useful option if a macro is not doing what you expect but you are not sure when the error is occurring.

- The **Edit** button lets you modify the macro (see page 238).

- The **Create** button is available when you type a new name in the **Macro name** box. This allows you to type in a new set of macro instructions.

- The **Delete** button removes a macro from the worksheet. You are asked for confirmation of the deletion.

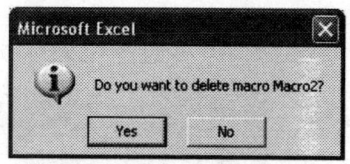

- The **Options** button displays a dialog box in which you can supply or change a shortcut key and change the macro description.

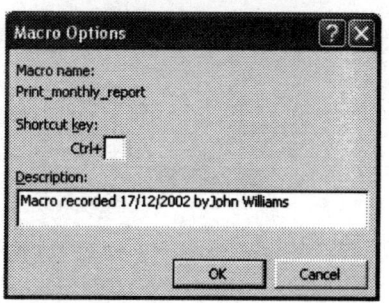

Add a macro to a toolbar

Buttons representing macros can be added to the toolbars, so that
the macros can be run by clicking on the buttons.

1 Use **Toolbars** from the **View** menu to display the toolbar to
which you want to add macro buttons.

2 From the **Tools** menu, select **Customize**.

3 Click on the **Commands** tab.

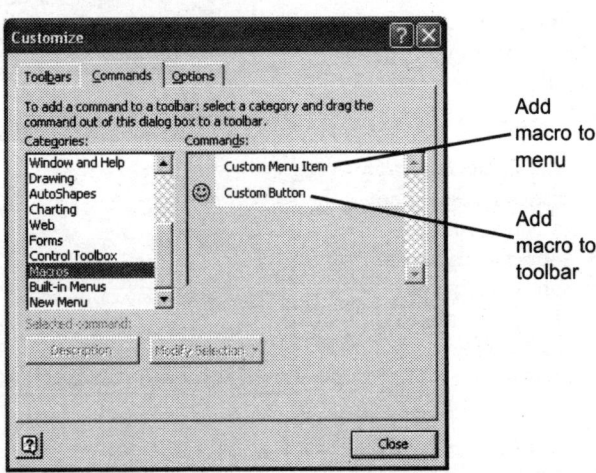

Add macro to menu

Add macro to toolbar

4 In the **Categories** box, click on **Macros**.

5 Drag the **Custom Button** to the toolbar.

6 Click on the **Modify Selection** button and then on **Assign Macro**.

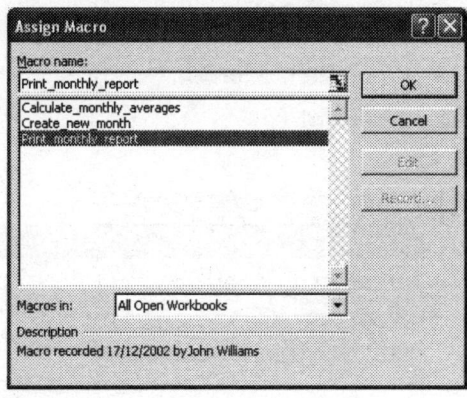

7 Click on a macro and then on **OK**.

8 Click on the **Modify Selection** button again and then on **Change Button Image**. Click on one of the supplied icons.

9 Repeat for any other macros to be added to the toolbar, then click on **Close**.

You can also drag the **Custom Menu Item** to a menu.

Add a macro button to a worksheet

Macro buttons can be inserted directly onto a worksheet.

1 From the **View** menu, select **Toolbars** and click on **Forms**.

2 On the Forms toolbar, click on the ▣ button.

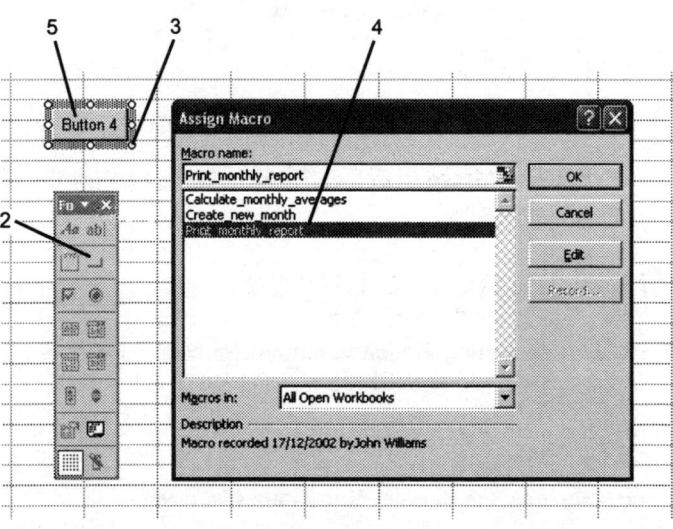

3 Mark out the area to be covered by the button.

4 In the Assign Macro dialog box, click on a macro name and then on **OK**.

5 Replace the button name by typing a new name.

When you click on the button, the macro is executed.

Change a macro button

To change the text on a macro button or assign a new macro:

1 Right-click on the button.

2 To change the button text, select **Edit Text** from the pop-up menu and then retype the text. To assign a different macro, select **Assign Macro** from the pop-up menu and choose the macro from the list.

Delete a macro button

To delete a macro button from a worksheet:

1 Right-click on the button.

2 Select **Cut** from the pop-up menu.

Set macro security level

If you load a workbook from floppy disk, CD or e-mail, you will also be loading any macros it contains. Some of these macros may contain viruses, so you need to protect yourself against them.

Macros containing viruses can be disabled by setting an appropriate security level.

1 From the **Tools** menu, select **Macro** and **Security**.

2 Click on the required level.

3 Click on **OK**.

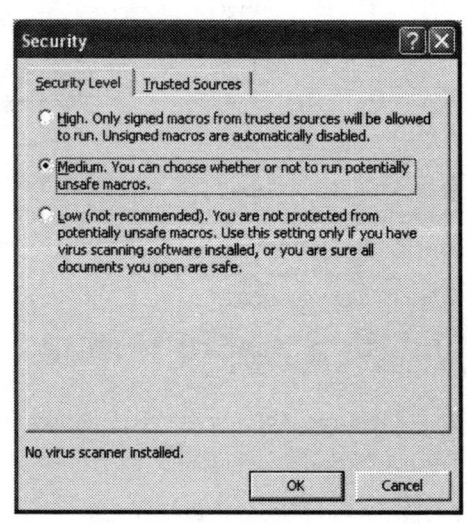

Security   ?X

Security Level | Trusted Sources

○ High. Only signed macros from trusted sources will be allowed to run. Unsigned macros are automatically disabled.

● Medium. You can choose whether or not to run potentially unsafe macros.

○ Low (not recommended). You are not protected from potentially unsafe macros. Use this setting only if you have virus scanning software installed, or you are sure all documents you open are safe.

No virus scanner installed.

OK   Cancel

17

exchanging data

Copy data between Excel worksheets

A block of data can be copied from one worksheet to another.

1 Mark the range to be copied and press **[Ctrl]** + **[C]**.

2 Open the second worksheet.

3 Click on the cell that is to be the top left-hand corner of the range and press **[Ctrl]** + **[V]**. The block is copied, including all display formatting.

Copy a table from Word or Access

Tables of data created in Word or parts of an Access database table can be copied across to an Excel worksheet.

1 In Word or Access, mark a block of data in a table and press **[Ctrl]** + **[C]**.

2 In Excel, click on the cell that is to be the top left-hand corner of the new range and press **[Ctrl]** + **[V]**.

Import a CSV file

Data from a comma-separated values (CSV) file can be used as the basis for an Excel worksheet.

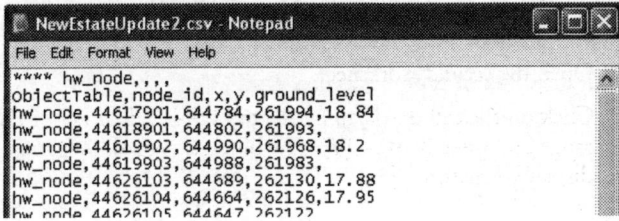

1 From the **File** menu, select **Open**.

2 In the **Files of type** box, select **Text Files**.

3 Click on a file with a CSV extension and then on **Open**.

Each line in the file becomes one row, with each item in the line being placed in a separate cell.

	A	B	C	D	E	F
1	**** hw_node					
2	ObjectTab	node_id	x	y	ground_level	
3	hw_node	44617901	644784	261994	18.84	
4	hw_node	44618901	644802	261993		
5	hw_node	44619902	644990	261968	18.2	
6	hw_node	44619903	644988	261983		
7	hw_node	44626103	644689	262130	17.88	
8	hw_node	44626104	644664	262126	17.95	

Import a text file

A text file containing data in a tabular format can be imported into Excel. This method is useful for importing data that has been output as a print file from some other application.

1 From the **File** menu, select **Open**.

2 In the **Files of type** box, select **Text Files**.

3 Click on a text file and then on **Open**.

4 The first step of the Text Import Wizard is displayed. Click on **Fixed Width** if the data is in a table or **Delimited** if data items are separated by commas or tabs. Click on **Next**.

5 Check that the column breaks are in the correct positions. The dividers can be dragged to new positions. Clicking on a gap adds a divider; double-clicking on a divider removes it. Click on **Next**.

tip

If the dividers are not in the right positions or are missing, this is usually an indication that somewhere in the data there is a row where there is a problem with column spacing.

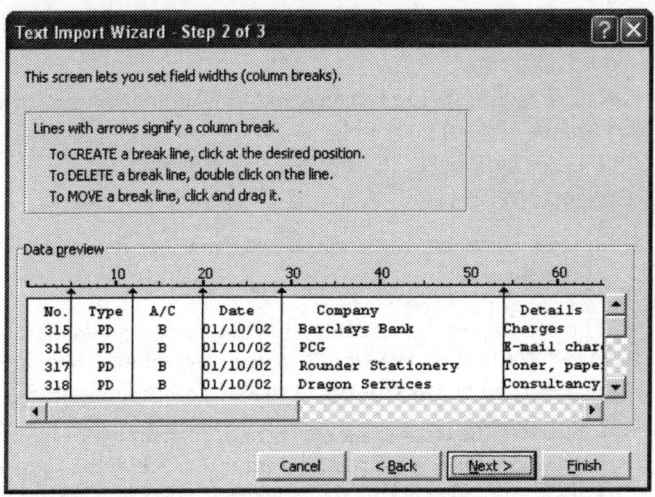

6 Set the display format for each column. Click on **Finish**.

The data is imported and can be formatted in Excel.

	A	B	C	D	E	F	G
1	No.	Type	A/C	Date	Company	Details	Amount
2	315	PD	B	01/10/2002	Barclays Bank	Charges	4.63
3	316	PD	B	01/10/2002	PCG	E-mail charges	80.00
4	317	PD	B	01/10/2002	Rounder Stationery	Toner, paper	350.00
5	318	PD	B	01/10/2002	Dragon Services	Consultancy	100.00
6	319	PD	B	28/09/2002	Post Office	Postage	11.01

Copy a range to Word or Access

A range of Excel data can be copied into a Word document or an Access table.

1 In Excel, mark the block of data to be copied and press **[Ctrl] + [C]**.

2 In Word, move the cursor to the point at which you want to import the table; in Access, open a table and mark a range of the same size as the Excel range.

3 Press **[Ctrl] + [V]** to paste the data.

Data from Excel can also be copied to many other applications using this method.

Copy an Excel chart to another application

An Excel chart can be copied to any other application that displays pictures.

1 In Excel, click on the chart and press **[Ctrl] + [C]**.

2 In the other application, click and press **[Ctrl] + [V]**.

Export a worksheet to a text file

An Excel worksheet can be saved as a text or CSV file, which is then suitable for import to many other applications. You can only save one worksheet at a time in text format.

1 Save the file in its current format.

2 From the **File** menu, select **Save As**.

3 In the **Save as type** box, select either **Text** or **CSV**.

4 Type a name for the file and click on **OK**.

5 You are warned that only the current worksheet will be exported. Click on **OK**.

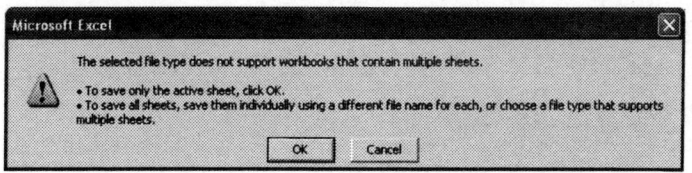

6 You are warned that any formatting will be lost. Click on **OK**.

Add a hyperlink to a Web page

You can insert a link to a site on the Internet.

1 Click on the cell that is to contain the link.

2 From the **Insert** menu, select **Hyperlink**.

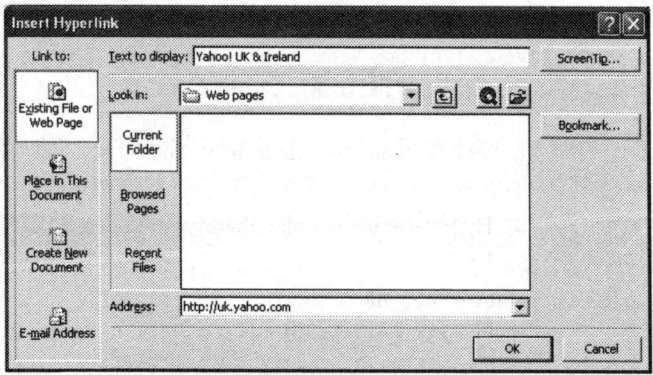

3 Type in the address of the link.

Or

Click on the 🔍 button, locate the page in your browser and then close the browser.

4 In the **Text to display** box, type the text you want to appear in the cell (which will be underlined).

5 Click on **OK**.

When you click on the hyperlink, the browser is loaded and the Web page is displayed.

Internet links	
Search:	Yahoo! UK & Ireland
Home:	AOL

Copy data from a Web page

A table of data can be copied from a Web page into Excel. There are two ways of doing this, depending on how the data is stored in the Web page.

To make a copy of a table from a Web page:

1 Display the Web page in your browser.

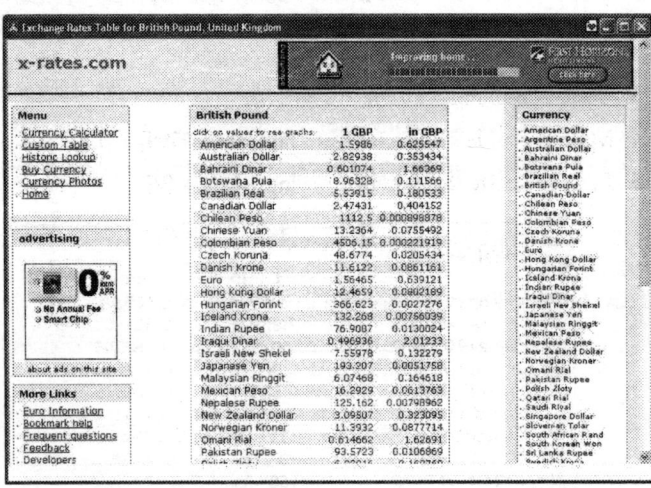

2 Mark the table and press **[Ctrl] + [C]**.

3 In Excel, click on the cell that is to be the top left-hand corner of the new range and press **[Ctrl] + [V]**.

If this method is unsuccessful (resulting in data that does not form a neat table in Excel), you can overcome the problem by saving the original HTML file:

1 Display the Web page in your browser.

2 From the browser's **File** menu, select **Save As**. Specify that the page is to be saved as an HTML file and save it using the default name or a name of your own.

3 Open Word and load the HTML file.

4 Mark the table of data in Word and press **[Ctrl] + [C]**.

5 In Excel, paste the data by pressing **[Ctrl] + [V]**.

	A	B	C	D
1	**British Pound**			
2		1 GBP	in GBP	
3	American Dollar	1.5986	0.625547	
4	Australian Dollar	2.82938	0.353434	
5	Bahraini Dinar	0.601074	1.66369	
6	Botswana Pula	8.96328	0.111566	
7	Brazilian Real	5.53915	0.180533	
8	Canadian Dollar	2.47431	0.404152	
9	Chilean Peso	1112.5	0.000898878	
10	Chinese Yuan	13.2364	0.0755492	
11	Colombian Peso	4506.15	0.000221919	
12	Czech Koruna	48.6774	0.0205434	
13	Danish Krone	11.6122	0.0861161	

Publish a worksheet on the Web

A worksheet can be saved as an HTML file in a format suitable for uploading to a Web site.

1 Save the Excel file, then select **Save As** from the **File** menu.

2 In the **Save as type** box, select **Web Page**. Choose to publish either the entire workbook or just a selection on the current worksheet. Click on **Publish**.

3 Select the range to publish. Decide whether to add spreadsheet functionality (allowing users limited options for features such as sorting of data). Click on **Change** and give the sheet a title. Enter a

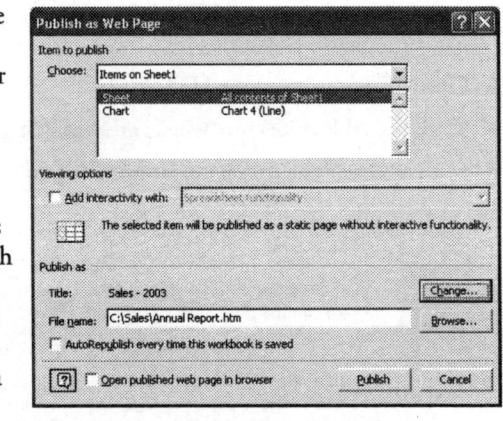

filename (including a location). Click on **Publish**.

An HTML file is created, with relevant files in a subdirectory.